The Things You Should Know About Sex but Don't

A guide for men and women that makes sense

Steven Roode

Acknowledgement:

To Alicia,

For making me sane again and bringing me back from a very low point in my life. For taking the time to show me there is such a thing as real love, and even real love can be kinky. For bearing with me through the countless revisions of this book and having to hear all of my sexual experiences with other partners (I know that was not easy).

I also want to thank her for supporting me through all my crazy ideas. Even while going to college, building robots, starting a company, and having breakdowns. For never doubting me, always encouraging me to finish this book, and most of all loving me for who and what I am. Thank you for everything you have done Alicia.

All other names in this book have been changed so no one is mistaken, embarrassed, or hurt. Discretion is the better part of valor, and even though I am describing sexual encounters I will not specify times or names that could lead back to the wonderful men and women who gave me the experiences and inspiration to write this book. This book is for all of them.

Contents

Forward:..3

Introductions: 7

Chapter 1: In the Mind...9

Chapter 2: Language and Stereotypes...16

Chapter 3: Making Love, Having Sex, and Fucking 22

Chapter 4: Age Difference vs. Maturity 29

Chapter 5: Masturbation 36

Chapter 6: Oral Sex 41

Chapter 7: Anal 47

Chapter 8: Toys 55

Chapter 9: Toppings...60

Chapter 10: Simple Bondage 66

Chapter 11: Advanced Bondage 73

Chapter 12: Degradation and Humiliation..82

Chapter 13: Building Your Own Play Room 86

Chapter 14: Voyeurism and Exhibitionism 92

Chapter 15: Threesomes and More..99

Chapter 16: Swinging..105

Chapter 17: An Act too Far 110

Conclusion 114

Glossary 116

Bibliography 118

Forward:
By Alicia

When Steven first told me that he was writing a book about his sexual experiences, I was both intrigued and apprehensive at the same time. It was not that I believed he did not have something valuable to say. Rather, I believed that my limited experiences added little value to the equation. Reading through the book had me question on multiple levels the sum of what I added to his life. As intelligent and gifted as I am, I suffer from what many people do, an apprehension based upon a lifetime of unsatisfying experiences.

Let me explain, my entire sexual experience prior to meeting Steven can be summed up in terms of a pitiful amount of minutes. I found that the "play" was always the same. In a bed, they would roll over, pat me twice, grab somewhere once, less than 2 minutes later roll back over and game over. There was little intimacy, less romance, and zero trust.

Sex was an autopilot function for the individuals I was with, more about them and their 30 seconds of fame rather than about any type of connection. I started to experience tremendous amounts of pain and I would avoid sex whenever possible. The more I was with someone; the less I could stand being with them because I stopped believing that they cared about me at all.

In the end, all relationships rely and depend on trust. From simple one night stands to the most extreme sexual encounters, there is a confidence in understanding each other's expectations. As I read Steven's first versions of the book, I commented on this many times. The situations where he believed he was providing an ultimate experience for someone, when in fact he did or could have brought him or her greater harm. The times when it seemed like it was more about checking off a list instead of caring anything at all about the other individual. In essence, like everyone I had been with before, all about him and not about the connection, thankfully Steven is not like that.

I do feel; however, that his experiences are important for individuals to understand. Sex is more than checking the block. It is more than just an encounter. Sex is a connection based upon confidence in yourself, and absolute faith that your partner understands your needs and will never betray you.

When you are with someone, you give more than just your body, no matter what kind of relationship you have. We talked a lot about this as he made subsequent changes to the book, and I believe that the greatest take away anyone can get is that sex is all about trust.

Betrayal in any form may seem like the easiest answer. Have your cake and eat it too after all this is the rule we are taught early on. However, the little lies we tell the people we love, the things we hide from them, deceits no matter how small; they erode at a relationship until there is no room left for intimacy. Do not ever believe that your loved one does not know your secrets. Lies, deceit, and manipulation will damage intimate relationships permanently. Master the art of an open and honest relationship and the intimacy that follows will blow your mind.

If either person is unclear on this, there will be mixed expectations and someone will get hurt. Mistrust will shatter the offended party for future experiences and it will be that much harder for them to build a connection with their next intimate encounter, eventually making it impossible to establish a deep emotional bond with a significant other in an enduring relationship. You may not care; in fact, some may even find it an amusing game that is until it happens to you. The Things You Should Know About Sex but Don't gives you the rules you need to understand so that you can have amazing experiences. The rest is up to you; whether it is a string of one-night stands, something deeply personal, or as you transition through life a mixture of both.

Being with Steven has been an amazing salve to my soul. When I am with him, an emotional connection accentuates the physical in ways that are hard to describe. Even with all of his physical experiences, the emotional aspect he brings allows me to believe that he will always keep me foremost in his thoughts. That my needs, wants, desire, and safety are his primary concern; as are his to me.

Trust though comes at a cost; it takes communication with your partner. One partner may want something that goes beyond the comfort or safety level of the other. One individual may believe they need something that will actually cause them greater damage down the road. False expectations may arise when you are with someone so intimately that they mistakenly believe the experience to be something that it is not. Be clear up front about what you want from each individual you wish to be with.

It took a great deal of courage to read these experiences and not believe that Steven missed the variety to which he had become accustomed to in his life. It took strength, to not look at my past and ask myself what he got out of our relationship and not just in terms of intimacy. However, his life and experiences led him back to me and he has always been exactly the person I needed in my life.

We all take something from everyone we have been with, and for me everyone has taught me to be wary of relationships. With Steven though, from the first time I met him, an angry, hostile, and frustrated woman, to the day he came back into my life saying he had never forgotten me, I was always hypersensitive to issues of trust, and it was in fact paramount to anything else. My body and soul responds to him in ways I never thought would be possible. It is my hope that when you read these pages you will understand how the true rules of intimacy will enhance the most endearing of all of your encounters.

Always practice safe sex, be safe, be sane, consensual; keep your partner's needs first and foremost in your mind, and each encounter will be a positive and enjoyable one. Do not ever jeopardize yourself or your partner in any way for any reason.

Introductions:

I would like to explain how this book is broken down and why I say or write different parts different ways, and a little about whom I am. My name is Steven Roode and for the last 16 years, I have dedicated myself to learning and immersing into as much about the human sexual experience as possible. I am 34 years old, 5'10, in very good physical shape, and thoroughly enjoy the human body. I have traveled all across America and to several other countries around the world.

I recently started my own company called Adult Consulting For You, LLC, to instruct, demonstrate, and perform live arts rope displays based upon shibari and fusion styles. This is done in an environment free of pornography and nudity; where the models or customers are fully clothed. The goal is to teach individuals in a safe and non-threatening environment where the addition of these arts can enhance a relationship.

I have always been fascinated with the act of sex, as well as all the foreplay, and after play that goes along with it. Every experience with a partner that I have had meant something to me and I always tried to take a lesson away from it. Even one night stands or random encounters left their mark (sometimes literally) on me.

I have read a few good books and many bad ones on the subject of sex. The one thing that stands out most to me is the lack of good guides or even common sense rules to sex that a great deal of men and women just do not seem to get. It seems most books are just reruns of the Kamasutra, full of photos and little else or glorified sexual experiences with no context. This book is neither.

It is rather embarrassing because I consider myself a fairly smart person yet I do not see how most people fail to grasp these concepts. I want to share my knowledge and experiences with as many people as possible to hopefully make them better physical and mental lovers or at least more aware of their partners.

Throughout this book, each chapter is broken down into categories. I will give several paragraphs about each subject. Following will be a short story or series of stories from my personal experience on the subject both good and bad. Next, I will give you some psychological insight into the subject from various doctors who are considered experts in their fields. After this will be a series of rules, do's and don'ts for men and women that should be common sense but sometimes people just do not know or do not put forth the effort.

It is my sincere hope that you enjoy reading this book as much as I have enjoyed finally penning it to paper. The experiences over the course of my life have been extraordinary and I consider myself fortunate. I want to share these experiences to teach, not to brag.

"I am not trying to reinvent the wheel, only make the ride a little

smoother"- Steven Roode

Chapter 1: In the Mind

This chapter is dedicated to helping strengthen the mind and keep you mentally healthy when it comes to sex. I want to try and really impress upon the reader how much goes into each sexual act; be it alone masturbating, or in a full on swing party and everything in between. Each chapter of your sexual life has its own memories and experiences that come together to form your sexual self-identity.

Understanding how you evolve sexually benefits your mental health. Even the worst moments in your life can have a positive outcome. You can also overcome a traumatic event with the right partner carefully exploring the negative experience and finding ways to make future sexual experiences positive. Without the bad in our lives, we would never know how good something could be.

No matter what has happened in your life, with the right partner anything is possible. Make yourself happy and everything else will fall into place. Never be ashamed of your desires, just be careful how you act upon them.

That last sentence is key to my point, if it is legal, safe for you and your consenting partner, and feels good, why should you feel ashamed? Never be ashamed of who and what you are, nor what you enjoy; however, do not sacrifice your mental and physical health or anyone else's just for the sake of pleasure.

Keep in mind that the following ideas from Doctor Sigmund Freud are over 50 years old and the ideas and theories of sexual psychology have evolved since. However, if you want to understand all aspects of sexuality, it is good to know where the field began. As such, Dr. Freud was a giant in the field during his time.

Sigmund Freud developed a theory of how our sexuality starts from an early age and evolves through various fascinations. If these stages of psychological development are not completed at the right developmental times, they can trap us and they may lead to various defensive mannerisms later in life to avoid the distress produced from the issues in that stage (Freud, 1962).

These fixations, psychologically speaking; theorized that if the nursing child was denied during early stages of development, the anxiety could become an adulthood obsession otherwise known as a functional type of mental disorder (Freud, 1962). Therefore, a young child's desire would show itself as a fixation with oral stimulation; Yet if the child is weaned at an inappropriate stage of the time line, the child could be psychologically stunted due to the emotional conflicts at this stage of psychosexual growth and the child might develop an improper form of oral fixations later in life (Freud, 1962).

The child who is either under or over fed during the course of being breast-fed could become an orally fixated person. This fixation can have a couple different effects: First, the child who is neglected could become a psychologically dependent person always seeking that oral stimulus that was denied in early childhood, thereby becoming a devious and manipulative individual in fulfilling his or her needs, rather than growing to independence (Freud, 1962). Secondly, this over-protected child might not even want to become a functional adult, depending instead on others to fill their needs (Freud, 1962).

According to Freud's work, oral-stage fixations can manifest in ways such as, continual need of oral stimulation i.e. eating, smoking, chewing gum and or candy, and alcoholism. Clinically, these symptoms can include sarcasm, oral sadism, and or sexual practices to include fellatio, cunnilingus, and analingus (Freud, 1962). People who constantly chew on their lip or the inside of their cheeks are also noticeable oral fixations found commonly in people.

Freud's psychology points towards the human drive for sex, which is the basis of human survival on an evolutionary level, motivating man by the need for sexual reproduction. A strong sex drive is very positive aspect for the human species, and men and women that have a strong sex drive would have an evolutionary advantage over others. This would allow our ancestors to leave their genetic heirloom behind allowing the human beings to continue on.

Humans desire to have children could then be connected to Dr. Freud's explanation of man's desire to reproduce (Freud, 1962). This means that humanities sexual proclivities is not about sex alone, but intercourse with the desire of reproduction. Freudian psychology and its highlighting of the sex drive are very similar to evolutionary psychology which considers the sexual and aggressive drives as an imperative for survival of a person's genetic line and humanity in general (Freud, 1962).

Humanities basic needs for companionship, love, and stability are all aspects of these theories. The desires for building and creation has origins in sexual desire and the artistic work itself could be considered as an act of copulation according to psychoanalysis (Roy, 2008).

Men want many women to spread their genetic material farther. However, they generally do not prefer women with other men's children as they detract from resources to their possible offspring. Women, on the other hand want, strong prosperous men committed to them and their offspring's well-being and survival at the expense of any other children (Raine, 2013). This of course is at the most primitive thought processes regarding our evolution as a species.

The bulk of men under the age of 60 have sex on their mind at least once a day, according to Laumann, yet only one in four women admit they contemplate sex that frequently (Sex Drive: How Do Men and Women Compare?, 2014). As men and women get older, the fantasizing usually becomes less prevalent, but men still romanticize about sexual acts twice as much. One survey conducted by Roy Baumeister , a social psychologist at Florida State University, compared men and women's sex drives, found that men reported more spur-of-the-moment sexual excitement and more numerous and diverse fantasies than women (Sex Drive: How Do Men and Women Compare?, 2014).

"Men want sex more often than women at the start of a relationship, in the middle of it, and after many years of it," Baumeister concludes after reviewing several surveys of men and women (Sex Drive: How Do Men and Women Compare?, 2014). This is also true for gay and lesbian couples; the male couples reported having more sex more often than the female couples did at all stages of their relationships. Men admitted to wanting more sexual partners then women on average in their lifetime, and appear to be more interested in spontaneous sexual encounters as well (Sex Drive: How Do Men and Women Compare?, 2014).

Now I am not attacking any religions or the devout of their faith at all. I have my religion and my partners have their own. However, I found the next statistics fascinating, and the fact that this kind of survey was even conducted very interesting.

Female clergy do a healthier job of satisfying their vows of chastity than male clergy. Baumeister cited a survey of several hundred clergy in which 62% of male clergy admitted to being sexually active, in relation to 49% of female clergy (Sex Drive: How Do Men and Women Compare?, 2014). These same male clergy also reported more partners on average than the female clergy as well.

I think that everyone will agree that men and women function in a different way. This is particularly true in terms of our mental and emotional thinking. The reading on the difference between the sexes suggests that one of the reasons for this is the variances in the thought processes between the sexes.

Generally, men are more straightforward, they go from one place to another in the shortest line possible. Of course, women tend to think on a much larger scale, considering more of the world at a time. Of course, this generates different struggles due to communication issues from the cognizance of emotional accessibility, to their sexuality, even thought processes (Michael J. Formica, 2009).

Men are, by nature, physical beings. We are hunters' genetically. We evolutionarily and classically associate accessibility of a mate with their presence in the area. Generally the idea is simple, there is no mystic or special power in this; our DNA holds all the answers (Michael J. Formica, 2009).

Men are physical first, when dealing with adversaries and potential mates, and emotional after. The carnal accessibility of our mate points to sexual and emotional convenience and, since this is biological and expected to be something that we, the hunters often mistake causing disadvantages in relationships that do not automatically feel the need to interconnect with our intended partner (Michael J. Formica, 2009).

Women, in contrast, are reflective and complicated beings. Females keep just about every aspect of this world operating, and more often think about the entire situation, not just what's right in front of them (Michael J. Formica, 2009). For women, being physically aroused comes more from their emotions then physical desire itself. In that, emotional availability activates their physical availability, in saying, women's association with that partner arouses their sexual desire (Michael J. Formica, 2009).

In conclusion, women have the tendency to show up in the flesh and sexually when their partner engages them on an emotional level, while men generally present themselves physically, an emotional connection being stimulated after the encounter. You can see how these situations might cause conflicts and confusions, from the unobtainable mandate that male partners must be mind-readers; to the lifelong frustration of women with the seemingly widespread thoughtlessness of males that females must deal with (Michael J. Formica, 2009).

Rules for men:

1. Engage your partner emotionally, or at the very least play with your partner's mind as much as their body. Keep arousing them in that way, do not let your partner's mind wander and get bored or sidetracked.

2. Talk to your partner; do not ask every few minutes if they likes it, if they came, or how well you are pleasing them. That will make you seem insecure, childish, and not confident in yourself or your abilities.

   However, find a way to connect and keep that connection.

Rules for women:

1. Trigger your partner's imagination. The reason why a lot of partners prefer skimpy cloths, rather than straight out nudity all the time is the way it triggers the imagination. When a woman wears something skimpy, it draws attention to the areas a sexual partner most desires.

   This stimulates their imagination, because something is concealed.

   This increases our desire to see what is underneath.

2. You can also do things like suggesting that something good will happen later that night. Talk dirty to your partner. It does not need to be overtly sexual or wild. That will stimulate your partner mentally, and they will spend a good deal of time thinking about what you said, their imagination will do the rest of the work.

Chapter 2: Language and Stereotypes

In this chapter, I will discuss and demystify many of the "taboo" terms and ideas associated with unconventional sex such as the word taboo itself. Many people are unaware of the true meanings of certain words and phrases, and the acts that go along with them. For example, simply because someone says they are a Dominate or submissive individual does not mean their some sort of deviant freak, sex addict, or whore in any way.

Some people do not even know what they are, just that they were told what they were, and they saw it in a movie or read it from a book so they must be in that "niche." More often than not people "float" between these parameters and enjoy a little of everything.

BDSM is a wide umbrella term used to cover a large range of unconventional sexual acts and beliefs. BDSM stands for bondage and discipline, domination and submission, sadism and masochism. This is a combined acronym, which is thrown around a lot but does indeed cover a wide array of subjects. There is such a large diversity of practices, a portion of these may be enjoyed by individuals who may not categorize themselves as actively involved with BDSM, or presence in the BDSM scene at all. The presence in the BDSM community or subculture is mostly reliant on self-identification and collective experiences. There is no membership card or secret handshake. Curiosity in BDSM can be a variety from a single event experience to an entire lifetime of activities.

Terms like "play" and "host" are used throughout this book because it is just that, most of us (not stale, boring, average people) in varying degrees have "unusual" sex lives, enjoy it, and sexual encounters can be considered a game. You cannot take life too serious and sex provides the perfect time to play (safely please).

The host is generally a strong confident personality, a person who throws parties or organizes functions. That person you can count on to facilitate a great evening and fun environment. Even a couple can share this responsibility very well and help strengthen an already well-developed bond.

Sometimes a Dominate is someone who spends their day in a menial job or life and wants to feel empowered or in charge. The reverse can be said for a submissive, in their daily life they are generally powerful people or high-level employees that spend their lives telling others what to do. When it comes time to play, submissive partners may want to remove all that responsibility and weight off their minds.

There is generally a bell curve to that for both dominate and submissive lives. The more power they have, the more they want to surrender and vice versa. By no means is this the law, Dominance or submission can take many forms and crosses all lifestyles.

There is also another type for both the Dominate and submissive. For some the lifestyle is full time. People in power radiate confidence and enjoy being the alpha personality. Submissive personalities are drawn to them, seeking the safety and comfort of a Dominate partner.

Having to ask your partner for permission to talk to someone else, go shopping, and getting dressed and undressed, or even when you can use the bathroom throughout the day. These are your more traditional pure master and slave personalities. This aspect can be minimal to maximum with hundreds of variations in between. This by any means is not an all-inclusive list, merely some examples.

Keep in mind as well that this is not a male Dominate, female submissive society. Either one can be in charge; this is a sexist free environment. There are some instances, where two Dominate partners can get together for fun. However, I have never seen a relationship like that without a third partner; the submissive involved balancing out their needs for control.

Taboo to me is more of a joke, so many levels and degrees of this lifestyle that you cannot fit a person into a neat little box (unless they are a gimp) or category. Individuals who enjoy more risqué forms of sexual intimacy seem to be more free and happy with far less shame or regret then the average person. Humans fear the unknown and religions preach about us as sinners but the list of closet sins most "holy" people commit make it comical. It is like the kettle calling the pot black, the difference is to not judge from up on high.

The following terms are defined by Webster's dictionary followed by my own interpretation of the word.

1. Taboo- adjective \tə-ˈbü, ta-\: not acceptable to talk about or do. Something banned on grounds of morality or taste (Merriam-Webster's Dictionary and Thesaurus, 2014). The subject is taboo.

   My definition- Things that are done out of the ordinary of society. That is unknown to the average person.

2. **Dominatrix- noun \ˌdä-mi-ˈnā-triks\: a woman who controls and hurts her partner during sexual activity in order to give her partner sexual pleasure (Merriam-Webster's Dictionary and Thesaurus, 2014). My definition- It can be either a man or woman in the dominant roll, not just who is a top and who is a bottom, additionally who is the alpha in a group or partnership. Most often referred to as the "Dom"**

3. **Submissive- adjective \-ˈmi-siv\ : willing to obey someone else. Characterized by tendencies to yield to the will or authority of others (Merriam-Webster's Dictionary and Thesaurus, 2014).**

   My definition- This person wants complete release from decision making and control. It is like free falling but with sexual tones. Also known as the "sub" Notice that a Dom is always capitalized and the sub is never.

4. **Switch (I was unable to find a suitable official dictionary term) - someone who enjoys being both the Dominant or submissive at different times and in different situations in a relationship. A switch can be in an exclusive relationship or portray different roles with different partners. This term is not found in the dictionary in our context.**

5. **Bondage- noun \ˈbän-dij\ : the state of being a slave, sexual activity that involves tying a person up for pleasure . Sadomasochistic sexual practices involving the physical restraint of one partner (Merriam-Webster's Dictionary and Thesaurus, 2014).**

My definition- to bind, this can either be the psychological ownership of a partner as in with D&s relationships or the physical restraint with rope, leather, chains, or other materials that can hold a person in place or position.

6. Deviant- adjective \-ənt\ : different from what is considered to be normal or morally correct (Merriam-Webster's Dictionary and Thesaurus, 2014).

   My definition- anything that society does not allow or do on a regular bases. These deviances change with time. Stereotype and prejudice hold sway over this subject.

7. Sadomasochist- noun \ˌsā-(ˌ)dō-ˈma-sə-ˌki-zəm, ˌsa-, -ˈma-zə-\ : sexual behavior that involves getting pleasure from causing or feeling pain. The derivation of pleasure from the infliction of physical or mental pain either on others or on oneself (Merriam-Webster's Dictionary and Thesaurus, 2014).
   My description- S&M, the mother of "bad" when it comes to the bedroom. So very misunderstood due to its constant connection with serial killers and serial rapists. The adrenaline released and the chemical responses from the brain during pain/pleasure can be euphoric, thus the desire for it.

8. Voyeurism- one obtaining sexual gratification from observing unsuspecting individuals who are partly undressed, naked, or engaged in sexual acts; broadly: one who habitually seeks sexual stimulation by visual means (Merriam-Webster's Dictionary and Thesaurus, 2014). My definition- A person who enjoys watching others have sex with their permission. Gaining gratification through the acts of others

9. **Exhibitionism- A perversion in which sexual gratification is obtained from the indecent exposure of one's genitals (as to a stranger) b: an act of such exposure, the act or practice of behaving so as to attract attention to oneself (Merriam-Webster's Dictionary and Thesaurus, 2014).**

   My definition- I consider the act of enjoying being watched during sexual acts as exhibitionism, not those creepy people who flash children.

10. **Libido- noun \lə-ˈbē-(ˌ)dō also ˈli-bə-ˌdō\ : a person's desire to have sex Instinctual psychic energy that in psychoanalytic theory is derived from primitive biological urges (as for sexual pleasure or self-preservation) and that is expressed in conscious activity: sexual drive (Merriam-Webster's Dictionary and Thesaurus, 2014).**

    My definition- How much you want sex, how often you can have sex, and the amount of physical reaction your body has towards sex.

Chapter 3: Making Love, Having Sex, and Fucking

I am a firm believer that all forms of sex can be broken down into these three basic categories. Of course, there are variations upon these; however, generally all acts will fit into one of these categories. By no means should one act be limited exclusively and can fluidly shift to either of the others.

Even bondage, spanking, and other alternatives to sex can be done with lovemaking in mind. I have had experiences that left me mentally drained and satisfied on levels that cannot be compared with simple penetration. Any form of sexual pleasure can be loving, sexy, or fucking in nature.

As stated by the philosopher Alan Goldman "sexual desire is the desire for contact with another person's body and for the pleasure that such contact produces. Sexual activity is the activity that tends to fulfill such desire of your partner" (WEBMD, 2014).

According to Goldman, sexual activity is not automatically used as any further end (WEBMD, 2014). For instance, having a child is not the necessary drive for sexual intercourse; this negates committing anything wrong if you are being sexually active without attempting impregnation. Undeniably, Goldman goes on to elaborate; having sex is merely a fulfillment for humans need to physically bond with a partner (WEBMD, 2014).

Making love is the slow, passionate, caressing, emotionally charged experience. Making love is more than just a physical bond; it involves a deep spiritual and emotional connection that you will not experience with any other encounter. Often this produces the most intense sexual and psychological experiences. This type of encounter goes far beyond the physical act alone.

Just as important as the act of lovemaking, is of course the time spent afterwards. Holding each other, lightly petting and whispering in your partner's ear finishes that bond between you. This is a big difference from the other two types of intercourse.

Having sex is the in between, it can be a hasty trip to the bathroom with a friend or good night sex with a glass of wine. There is more passion and less slow movements. It is not quite making love and its light for fucking. This is more in the realm of recreational, a good feeling to be shared with your partner.

Most encounters fall into this category. There is no preset notion before beginning and you both should get a form of satisfaction from sex. Satisfaction however, is not based upon orgasms and should not be kept on a scoreboard.

Now fucking… THAT is the all out, hard-core, sweat dripping down your body experience. This is when you and a stranger at a party look at each other from across the room and you both just know. You wind up in the bathroom ripping clothes off and just going at it without even saying a word. Even with a lover, this can be just as intense and powerful.

Fucking also includes when you have angry make up sex or heated passion beyond control with your partner or partners. Breaking the bed, leaving marks on the walls and furniture, and speaking unintelligently from loss of mental capacity are good examples of a job well done.

Any of these are perfectly fine and amazingly good for your mind and body. "Sexually active people take fewer sick days," says Yvonne K. Fulbright, PhD a sexual health expert (WEBMD, 2014). This well-being people experience during sexual pleasure lasts and echoes through out your day and week.

Sexually active people also tend to be healthier; having greater amounts of what protects your body against microorganisms, infections, and other intruders. Researchers at Wilkes University in Pennsylvania found that college students who had sex once or twice a week had higher levels of an infection fighting immunoglobulin A (IgA) versus others of similar age that were less sexually active (WEBMD, 2014). These immunoglobulins are found in areas of the body such as saliva and in the blood system.

"Having sex will make sex better and will improve your libido" says Lauren Streicher, MD (WEBMD, 2014). Dr. Streicher is an assistant clinical professor of obstetrics and gynecology at Northwestern University's Feinberg School of Medicine in Chicago. "Sexually active women tend to have increased vaginal lubrication, blood flow, and elasticity" she says, conversely making sexual activity feel better and increase the desire to have more sex (WEBMD, 2014).

Having a strong pelvic floor is vital in escaping incontinence; almost 30% of women will suffer at some point in their lives by this (WEBMD, 2014). Working out your pelvic floor is easily done by simply having quality sex. When women have an orgasm, the muscles in the pelvic area contract making them stronger (WEBMD, 2014).

Dr. Pinzone, MD says, "Research suggests a link between sex and lower blood pressure" (WEBMD, 2014). He found one breakthrough study that sexual interaction definitely lowered systolic blood pressure." That of course is the first of two numbers on your blood pressure test (WEBMD, 2014).

In most cases, systolic blood pressure is the more important number due to serious risk factors for cardiovascular disease in people especially from 50 and on. Systolic blood pressure increases progressively in most people as we age because of increasing rigidity in the large arteries, long-term build-up of plaque, and enlarged occurrence of cardiac and vascular diseases (WEBMD, 2014).

"Sex is a really great form of exercise" Pinzone says (WEBMD, 2014). Sex will not substitute running or other cardio, however, it does help. Intercourse burns an average of five calories per minute, much more per minute than watching TV. Sex is a nice way to bump up your heart rate and depending on the intensity, can use several muscle groups. Of course the more hardcore the sex, the more muscles used, the more calories burned.

So get busy! Keeping a regular sexually active calendar can be of great benefit to your health. "Like with exercise, consistency helps maximize the benefits" Pinzone says (WEBMD, 2014). Just please do not make it a monotonous choir, that will kill the whole point behind enjoying sex.

Your heart health and good sex go hand in hand. Setting aside the cardiovascular advantages, being sexually active helps balance your estrogen and testosterone levels. "When estrogen or testosterone is low you problems start to occur, like osteoporosis and even heart disease" Pinzone says (WEBMD, 2014). The sexual activity frequency during one study of men who had sex at least twice a week were 50% as likely to die of heart disease as men who abstained from sex.

"An orgasm can block pain" says Dr. Komisaruk, a well-known professor at Rutgers University in New Jersey (WEBMD, 2014). Sexual intercourse discharges a hormone that boosts your pain limits. This is a physical reason that some people can enjoy pain as pleasure.

Stimulation without orgasm can also do the trick. "We've found that women masturbating can block chronic back and leg pain, several women have informed the doctors that masturbation can reduce menstrual cramps, arthritic pain, and even headaches" Komisaruk says (WEBMD, 2014).

Ambardar says, "Touching and hugging can release your body's natural feel-good hormone" (WEBMD, 2014). Becoming sexually excited causes a chemical in the brain called dopamine, endorphins and oxytocin to fire up the pleasure and reward center. Sexual and intimate acts can increase your selfesteem and mental well being as well. It is a recommendation for a healthy, happy, and satisfying life.

David Weeks MD, lead researcher at the Royal Edinburgh Hospital in Scotland, published a book based upon a study called "Secrets of the Super Young", found that "the key ingredients for looking younger are staying active and maintaining a good sex life" (50+:Live Better, Longer Can Good Sex Keep You Young?, 2014). A study conducted of 3,500 people, with ages ranging from 30 to 101, Dr. Weeks discovered that sex helps appearance when viewed by a panel of independent and unbiased people. This panel found most the subjects were between four and seven years younger in appearance of photos (50+:Live Better, Longer Can Good Sex Keep You Young?, 2014).

So have sex, be healthy, look younger, and live longer.

Rules for men:

1. Take the time to make love. It is not always about how fast, and hard you can go, feel your partner's reactions. Your partner will tell you with their body what intensity they want.

2. One of the key rules of sex for men is to take things slow and make sure to warm your partner up before things get serious. Spending time kissing your partner, stroking your partner, caressing your partner and more will make sure that they feel like you are excited about being with them. Foreplay gentlemen, foreplay.

3. To be a good lover, you must be an unselfish lover. If your partner feels like you are just in it for your own satisfaction, they are not going to be happy, and is more than likely not going to want a repeat performance. However, if you take the time to take care of their needs, your partner will be very appreciative and will generously reward you in return. Leave an impression that will last.

4. If as soon as the sex is over you are getting dressed and heading for the door, your partner is going to feel used, cheap, and disappointed. Spend some time cuddling with them, holding them, and telling them how much you enjoyed your time together afterword.

5. Ensure that if you are not with a long-term partner that you are always practicing safe sex.

Rules for women:

1. Different for a man, with you it's all control with your body, like riding a horse, you can use your legs, hips, arms, and your entire body to tell your partner what kind of sex you are wanting.

2. Men love hearing what you want. Tell your partner to make love to you, have sex with you, or to fuck you. Your partner will not care how you say it; it is just nice to hear.

3. Remember to move! Ever been with a partner that just laid there? Do not turn into that one.

4. If you are not enjoying intercourse, say something… or change it up. It is supposed to be pleasure for both of you.

5. Ensure that you always have an effective and consistent form of birth control until you and your partner are ready to have children. Always practice safe sex if you have multiple partners. Women unfortunately suffer from more sexual health related issues than men and many can cause permanent damage.

Chapter 4: Age Difference vs. Maturity

A big issue I have been asked about on several occasions is the difference between the ages of partners. There are several opinions on chronophilia defined as (the sexual enjoyment of partners of a widely differing chronological age) whether you want to speak anthropologically or sociologically. My opinion and research is the only one I can speak to; however, if you are interested in the scientific answer then you will need to consult other books in a different section of a store than you will probably find this one. In this case, I have included some notes from credible sources here.

I never go below 18, it is a law, and as twisted as people think I can be I never do that one. However, before I was 18 I was with a few girls around my age, from about 15-18 but never lower than that, and the minute I turned 18 I never did again. This was due to my chosen profession in my early life.

I was 17 when I was with a wonderful woman who set me on the path of the sexual greatness I have achieved. She was a 47-year-old retired stockbroker from New York. At that point in my life I had only been with a handful of girls around my age. Now here was a woman! One who knew what she wanted and how she could get it.

I do see the hypocrisy in this, that she was 30 years older than me and that I said I would never be with someone under 18, but I was the one under 18 and I didn't have that rule till after I was 18. Everyone makes mistakes; the point is to learn from them.

We worked out a deal where she bought me a new Isuzu Rodeo and I would come see her a couple times a week. During those times, she would teach me so much. I have always said that every woman after her should thank her for all she taught me. Although please understand I realized later that what worked for her was not the hard and fast rules for every woman, every person you are with will desire different things. She was very patient and understanding of my teenage hormones and ADHD. She would instruct me on how she liked to be touched, made loved to, fucked, and everything in between. We covered a great deal of topics but none of it risqué.

She was still a proper woman, but one who had grown tired of the game and simply wanted a good lay from time to time. I was more than happy to accommodate this wonderful sexy woman. She was constantly telling me "do it like this, don't do that", how deep, how fast, and how long she liked her intercourse. I gained a lifetime of knowledge in only a few months with her.

On the other hand, I have been with women my age who were absolutely idiots. Age can be a difference when there are years between people, but maturity can overcome any number. Men and women who are unsure of anything in their lives, or what they want from a sexual partner are boring and frustrating to deal with.

There was a young woman who I enjoyed the company of immensely yet was only 22, and there have been women in their mid to late 30's who acted very immature and childish. Mental age and physical age can be as vastly different as the Grand Canyon and a swimming pool.

Being with older partners has its share of challenges though. You may misunderstand each other more because of a generation gap. You may face disapproval from others because of their ideology or upbringing. You may have to overcome differences in life philosophies and goals. Nevertheless, the connections that people can feel for each other are not bound by age, and being with an older person can open your eyes to different, more mature perspectives and experiences.

Keep in mind that the older your partner is (50+) the more consideration you might have to apply to sex. An example of course is the male erection, as men get older it becomes slightly less firm and can take longer for a man to achieve an erection. This is not an end all for men, just an average. There are all kinds of magic pills and devices to help along the way, but with practice and a little work, men can stay just as majestic and powerful as their earlier years without assistance in most cases.

For women generally the orgasm becomes less intense, and the vagina becomes less self-lubricated. Once again, this is not every woman everywhere, just a medical average. Simply bring a little lube and enjoy the night away. Age is not a restriction; nothing can compete with years of experience and a desire that never burned out.

Ultimately people desire the companionship of one another. Even as we reach our "silver" or "golden" years, most people still want to continue to have an active and enjoyable sex life. Now add in the fact that the kids are probably all out of the house and retirement may have come along, and free time is now abundant, there are no more excuses not to have sex with a loving partner.

Even with a perfect life, we still age, and with this aging of course comes inevitable physical changes (Sex and Aging, 2014). These changes can affect a person's capability to enjoy sexual intercourse or play with a partner (Sex and Aging, 2014). There are of course, men and women who enjoy sex even more as they age. For example, after menopause or a hysterectomy, women may no longer be concerned with becoming pregnant; they may feel more open to enjoy sex (Sex and Aging, 2014).

Most women whose hair has gone grey or that wrinkles have crept up on, do not believe they are less attractive, being confident and self-assured in their sexuality. Some women however, believe that they must be able to still have children or look young and "swim suit" attractive to be feminine, this may begin to cause anxiety about how desirable she is even before reaching that age (Sex and Aging, 2014). That can take away sexual enjoyment for her, keep this in mind, and be sensitive if needed.

Women may notice changes in their sexual organs. As women age their vagina shortens, narrows, and the walls become thinner and a little stiffer as well. This does not mean women cannot enjoy having sex at all; however, women generally have less vaginal lubrication as well (Sex and Aging, 2014). This could affect sexual pleasure, as long as you keep these concerns in mind there should be no problems (Sex and Aging, 2014).

Impotence is the most common problem sexually for men as they age. Impotence is the inability to have and maintain an erection hard enough for sexual intercourse (Sex and Aging, 2014). By age 65, about 15 to 25% of men are stricken with this difficult issue at least one out of every four times they are sexually active (Sex and Aging, 2014). Heart disease, high blood pressure, or diabetes can be contributing factors to impotence, due to the disease or because of the medication prescribed for them (Sex and Aging, 2014).

Men can find that it takes longer to achieve erection, erections may not be as strong or as large as they are used to, the volume of ejaculate can be smaller, reduction of erection following sexual activity (you get soft right after sex instead of staying hard for a while), or time before a new erection can be achieved after orgasm (Sex and Aging, 2014). Men may also find that they are in need of more foreplay or other stimuli. Another problem that can affect a man's erection at any age are certain types of antidepressants, but this too can be mitigated with the right partner.

A study conducted at Duke University published in the November 1974 Journal of the American Geriatrics Society found at age 68; almost 70% of men were sexually active on a regular basis. However, that number dropped to 25% by age 78 (Sex and Aging, 2014). A study from the January 1990 issue of the Archives of Internal Medicine, found that nearly 74% of married men and 56% of married women over 60 remain sexually active (Sex and Aging, 2014).

Sexual Interest and Behavior in Healthy 80 to 102-year-olds, a study published in the Archives of Sexual Behavior, April 1988, found that 63% of men and 30% of women were still sexually active (Sex and Aging, 2014). Cindy M. Meston, PhD, noted in "Aging and Sexuality," published in the October 1997 issue of the Western Journal of Medicine, "given that by the age of 80 or older there are 39 men for every 100 women, lack of opportunity may well account for a large portion of such gender differences" Dr. Meston said (Sex and Aging, 2014).

By no means, should this count you out, men and women both can carry on a healthy, strong, active sexual life throughout their golden years. Every partner is unique and must be treated as such. We all age differently and how well you take care of yourself will help how you age sexually. Proper diet and exercise can keep father time at bay as well.

Rules for men:

1.   Just because your partner is young and hot does not mean he or she will be good in bed, arm candy rarely makes up for dead weight in the sack.

2.   Just because they are older does not mean they are any wiser either, it is very hard to judge a sex book by its cover (pun intended).

3.   Don't count out any age, I have known an 81-year-old woman who still got very wet, and gave an amazing blowjob.

Rules for women:

1.   That grey haired silver back might be the stud of your dreams, or he could be a Viagra popping limp noodle who needs 24 hour notice before sex. Take it for a test drive before buying, maybe a little slap and tickle and see if you get a reaction from the pants before going all aboard only to find out that flag does not fly.

2.   Sometimes, you strike gold with a younger man with a rock hard body, and a penis that can go three or more times a night and is very enthusiastic. Just make sure he is not a moron in the head or he will never learn. Some are eager to please though.

3.   Trust your instincts; make sure you feel comfortable and safe. If there is a big difference in age then take it a little slow and feel each other out.

Chapter 5: Masturbation

First off, never be ashamed of masturbation. That should be a bold, underlined, 40-point font phrase but the editor would not let me… There is not a therapist out there who would tell you that when you were developing as a child into a teenager that it is not healthy to touch yourself sexually. I found a great article from (WEBMD) that I want to share here.

Masturbation is the self or partner assisted stimulus of the genitals to achieve sexual arousal and pleasure, usually to the point of orgasm (WEBMD, 2014). Most often, this is achieved by touching, stroking, or massaging the sexual organs of both men and women until an orgasm is achieved. Some men and women use sexual stimulation of the vagina or penis to masturbate or use sexually assistive devices such as a vibrator.

Masturbation is a rather common behavior, even among those who have regular sex partners. In one national study, 95% of males and 89% of females reported that they have masturbated (WEBMD, 2014). For just about all men and women masturbation is the first sexual act experienced. In young children, masturbation is a normal part of the individual's investigation of their own body. Most individuals continue to self-stimulate at all stages of their lives.

In addition to physical pleasure, masturbation is a great way to get rid of sexual tension that can build up over time, especially for people without a partner or when your partner is sexually unavailable, either through physical distance or just an emotional unavailability (WEBMD, 2014). A safe substitute for people wanting to avoid unplanned pregnancy or sexually transmitted diseases (STD's) includes masturbation (WEBMD,

2014). Masturbation is required for a man when giving a sperm sample for medical reasons. For cases of sexual dysfunction in an adult, masturbation can be recommended by a sex therapist to help a person unable to experience an orgasm or for those who ejaculate too soon (WEBMD, 2014).

Masturbation was once known as a sign of a mental health issue; however, masturbation is now considered normal. Masturbation is a healthy sexual activity in which the feeling of pleasant fulfilment is acceptable and safe. During your life, masturbation can be a great way to experience sexual pleasure and performed with or without a partner.

Masturbation is considered a problem when it prevents sexual activity with a willing partner, is performed in a public setting, or causes the individual significant mental distress (WEBMD, 2014). It may cause distress if the act is done compulsively (often related to past trauma or religious shaming associated with the sex act and intimacy) and or if it interferes with life and accomplishments. If you find yourself crying while masturbating, I recommend seeking professional help immediately as there may be underlying emotional or physical trauma that needs to be dealt with.

The medical and psychological community in general agrees that masturbation is a normal and innocuous expression of sexuality for both men and women. When masturbation is safely enjoyed and no injury or harm to the body occurs, it can be accomplished in reasonableness throughout an individual's lifetime as a part of normal sexual conduct. There are cultures and religions that oppose masturbation in general even labeling it as an immoral crime. These misconceptions often lead to individual's guilt or humiliation about their deeds (WEBMD).

I did it as a teen; I still do it as an adult. Even on days when I have sexual intercourse three or four times, I still want to masturbate. I do not always, but the desire is there. It is not that I want it instead of sex; which some of my partners have had a hard time understanding. My sex drive has just never diminished, as I got older, I just have better control of it.

When I masturbate, it is a physical need, not a mental or emotional connection without a partner. It can even feel like a chore sometimes, I just have to have a release and it is hard to find a partner that wants or can handle it so often each day. Do not always assume if your partner masturbates that they find you any less sexually appealing or attractive.

Masturbation can be a great form of foreplay and with oral stimulation can be a series of fun events in and of themselves. Even allowing a partner to watch you masturbate or watching your partner masturbate can be a full session of fun.

Partner assisted masturbation can be a wonderful experience for you and your partner, just keep in mind that it's hard for anyone to play with you the way you play with yourself. Communication with your partner is key. Talk to them before and during. When you are the partner performing keep an open mind, listen to your partner to help improve your technique with them.

Each person is different, their wants and needs during the act of masturbation are completely unique. Listen to them and ask them to communicate how they feel and how you can make them feel better erotically. However, do not assume your partner shares the same feelings about masturbation as you do, so talk about it beforehand to see if it can be a shared activity.

A great benefit is to allow your partner to watch you masturbate. Not only can this be an erotic session but allows your partner to see how and what you like at the same time. Share this experience and grow from it with your partner.

Sexual competency and sexual confidence begins with masturbation. In saying that, be comfortable with your own body before attempting to be comfortable with someone else's. Only once you have established trust and sureness with your own body, can you then trust others with your body or earn trust with someone else's body.

Rules for men:

1.   Never masturbate when you are sad, mad, or anxious. Masturbation should enhance a mood, not change it. If a pattern is created where sexual orgasm is connected with anger, sadness, or anxiety, this can cause significant problems in relationships and functioning. Let us say you consistently masturbate to relax when angry, and then you find yourself staying in a conflictual or maybe even abusive relationship because the sex is hot.

2.   If you get a rash, you are doing it too much. All good things turn bad when they are done too much. Just as they say about drinking, everything is fine in moderation excessiveness can be harmful. You should never miss important events or obligations for masturbation. If your schoolwork, relationships, or physical health is being compromised, you need to cut back.

3.   **Never sacrifice a relationship for masturbation**

Rules for women:

1. The most important thing you can do if you want to be sure that you climax when masturbating is first getting in the mood. Being in the proper mood helps make you a strong sexually healthy person.

2. If you have trouble reaching orgasm, or you just want to have a more pleasurable, sensual experience, then I strongly recommend using a lubricant of some kind. There are many different types of lube whether it is water based, oil based or made from something else. So make sure to experiment with each to find out, which you prefer, and to see which type helps to give you the strongest orgasms.

3. Do not get frustrated or give up if you have difficulty reaching orgasm, every woman's body is different, and react accordingly.

Chapter 6: Oral Sex

There are so many good ideas and intentions involved with oral sex. From both the giving and receiving side of oral sex can come great success or failures. I feel pity and a little anger towards the people that misuse or misunderstand oral sex. It is meant to be a joy for both partners; orgasm is not a primary concern, but a pleasant surprise. It should not be the goal to achieve orgasm as quickly as possible but to enjoy your partner.

Some common terms and slang used for oral sex include:

Fellatio, a BJ, becky, blowjob, bob on a knob, brain, deep throat, getting/giving head, gobble, hoover, a Lewinski, knob slobbing, playing the skin flute, smoking pole, sausage smoker, neck, drinking watermelon, and suck off are all related to sucking a dick.

Cunnilingus, eating out, going down, growling at the badger, muff diving, carpet munching, pink taco eating, motor boating the wet sea, eating pussy, going out for sushi, and clam smacking are all related to licking the vagina and
or clitoris.

I don't think I need to regale you with a tale about getting or giving head to make this chapter make sense, I'm fairly sure any person who reads this book has sucked a dick or eaten a pussy at least once in their life. However, I cannot lie that I feel no greater joy in life then having a woman sit on my face and grind her way to orgasm. The feel and taste of a woman brought to orgasm is second to none to me.

I have always made it a policy of mine that if a woman is too insecure to sit on my face than I cannot have a relationship with them. That lack of confidence is a turn off for me personally. This is also an early way before intercourse to see how well your partner takes care of their body. However, this certainly is not a hard and fast rule.

Just the same as a woman, I will call Joan, that would suck me off, and bring herself to climax without either of us touching her. She described it to me the same way I speak about oral sex; the excitement is in what you do to the other person. Joan would moan while my cock was in her mouth and then she would shudder and cum.

The mental thoughts and emotional feeling from pleasing your partner can lead to orgasm just as easily as physical contact. This is known as sympathetic responses in the mind. The mind produces feelings like the act from observation or thinking of the act.

As good as some experiences can be there are always the bad ones… this was one of my bad ones. I had been awake for over two days because of my job and a woman I was seeing at the time lived over two hours away but really wanted to see me, and I her. I drove with windows down, radio blaring, and pounding all the energy drinks I could stand just to make it.

When I arrived, it was straight into the bedroom we went. She undressed about as fast as I had seen a person ever undress. I immediately picked her up, threw her on the bed, and went down on her. The next thing I knew she was slapping me and telling me to get the hell out of her house. Apparently, I had fallen asleep and was snoring between her legs. Do not ever do this; your partner is unlikely to be forgiving or welcoming for a while.

Do not make oral sex a chore; if one of you is regularly giving oral sex without really wanting to, you have killed the joy and excitement of the act. Oral sex should be a desire, fun, sensual. Not a sigh, resignation, and hoping your partner will finish soon so you can stop. There is nothing worse than feeling obligated to give head with no reciprocation. I love just randomly diving at my girlfriend while she is busy doing something around the house and trying to eat her out.

When the stimulation is to a woman's clitoris or labia from her partner's mouth or tongue it is called cunnilingus. Sexual stimulation to a man's penis by his partner's mouth or tongue is known as fellatio. The pleasuring of both partners simultaneously through oral sex is commonly known as sixty-nine.

These sexual acts for women and men may involve either heterosexual or homosexual partners. While oral sex was, until very recently, frequently deemed by western culture a perversion, there is evidence from artifacts and artistic works that it seems to have been much more acceptable throughout history (Dr. Westheimer, 2000). Artistic representations from Asia and other parts of the globe tend to support the view that oral sex is not as uncommon a sexual act as some would believe. Statues and carvings within a religious context in India and represented in the Kamasutra have depicted oral sex along with many other variants of sexual activity (Dr. Westheimer, 2000).

Earlier sex manuals viewed oral sex as essentially a part of foreplay before penetration leading to climax and ejaculation. For many couples, oral sex represents just another method for sexual pleasure and the act can climax in orgasm and ejaculation without moving on to actual intercourse of the partner by their lover.

In the absence of adequate sexual education programs, most people in the past had to learn about oral sex from others, who may have been just as unknowledgeable. In this day and age, it is all over the internet in many forms. This only increases not decreases the need for proper sex education among our youth. Urologists have reported that some women, possibly influenced by the street term for oral sex, a "blow job" have inadvertently injured their male partners by blowing air into the urethra (Dr. Westheimer, 2000). Additionally, while the internet is a great source of information, in terms of sexual wellness it may cause medical issues; so always verify any information you get off the internet is both medically accurate and reasonable.

Recently, the slang expression "drinking watermelon" was explained to me, it is gaining popularity in young men and women due to rap lyrics and the deceptive manner of the term referring to the more formal expression of oral sex. The limitation of these terms to oral-genital contact appears to reflect the historical view that the norm for sex should focus on the genitals (Dr. Westheimer, 2000). While other forms of pleasure involving the tongue or mouth on areas of the body other than genitals were not previously considered as variants of oral sex, they of course are now (Dr. Westheimer, 2000).

Most people use their mouth and tongue to kiss and lick their partner all over there body. While there is no generally used term for this form of oral sex, there is an old term for kissing and licking the entire body including the genital areas: "going around the world" or "a tongue bath." The subject of oral sex is a good example of how our languages have not developed adequate and correct terminology for all aspects of human sexual behavior (Dr. Westheimer, 2000).

I have to quote Dr. Westheimer one more time here for this incredible peace of wisdom; Orgasms are like snowflakes. No two are alike, and they vary from woman to woman. Dr. Ruth says she is not certain that "multiple orgasms truly exist; again, there is that lack of research." However, she says, in women, there is usually a quiet moment right before it happens, a sign you should keep receiving pleasure until you have finished (Dr. Westheimer, 2000). "Some couples mistakenly stop at that point" says Dr. Ruth (Dr. Westheimer, 2000).

I think I have to disagree with Dr. Ruth on this one point and one point only. I do believe in multiple orgasms. They are elusive creatures but I have found a few partners that indeed have several orgasms within moments of the previous one. Most people need a moment to catch their breath, or are over loaded from an orgasm and unable to enjoy a second one so quickly. However, there are some women I have encountered who can roll right from one into another and seem to have seizure like movements from all the pleasure.

It is entirely possible for a man to achieve orgasm without ejaculation as well. With proper physical training, a man can enjoy orgasms similar to a woman in the effect of intense pleasure without having to stop sexual play.

Rules for men:

1. Never assume that what worked on one woman will work on every woman.

2. It's about more than just the clit, she has lots of parts, enjoy them all

3. Talk to her before, during, and after sexual intercourse. Women are mentally stimulated just as much if not more than physically.

4. When you are on the receiving end of any sexual gratification, let your partner feel the control. Make your partner feel like it is the best experience in your life. Guide your partner if they need it but do not just stop them or tell them it is bad.

Rules for women:

1. **Remember men are just kids and need our ego stroked as much as our body.**

2. **Tell us how good we make you feel, how great it is, keep us motivated.**

3. **Do not forget the balls!**

4. **Nibbling and playing is one thing but remember that some of those areas have sensitive skin and unless they are into the pain, it is probably not feeling as good as you think…(scraping teeth)**

Chapter 7: Anal

Heterosexual and homosexual anal sex has been around for millennia. Paintings and etchings from Japan, China, and Europe all depict men performing anal sex on women, as do ancient erotic drawings, sculpture, and pottery from the Mediterranean and South America (Ley, 2011). You can read stories about ancient Rome and other cultures of that period where homosexual behavior was practiced. In some Polynesian cultures, anal sex was practiced explicitly as a means of birth control.

Today, some adolescents regard anal sex as a means to prevent conception, regardless of increased risks for transmission of sexually transmitted diseases (Ley, 2011). Over the last few decades, anal sex rates in both men and women have risen. In the Fifties, anal sex was reported by fewer than fifteen percent of the population (Ley, 2011). Modern overall rates suggest that around a third of men have performed anal sex on a woman, and slightly fewer women have received anal sex (Ley, 2011). Individuals in their early twenties have the highest rates of these groups.

So many people get this one wrong. This particular subject can ruin a night or an entire relationship. Idiot men out there have ruined this for the rest of us. When done properly anal sex can be highly enjoyable for women as well as men. I will give testament to both giving and receiving anal, which sounds rather odd as I say it, but yes there have been a couple of occasions that I was the recipient of anal pleasure.

Let me get mine over with first because due to stereotyping heavily in our country the fact that I "received anal pleasure" is probably making people pause and wonder.

Nope I am not gay; however, I have absolutely no fight with the lifestyle, choices, or the people. Many of my friends are gay and proudly so. I have had the best times at drag bars, and have lived with three gay men before. They kept an amazing house and there was never any pressure or uncomfortable moments being straight in their home.

So there I was… This of course is the best way to start a tale of sexual experience. I spotted this amazingly hot woman, rock hard body, Hawaiian decent and long black hair. She was about my age, both of us in our midtwenties I believe, at a bar. She was working there as a waitress, and I was drinking and shooting pool along with my mouth at her. She bit and it seemed she was about as sexually open as I was.

Basically, that means we were about thirty seconds from fucking right there in the bar. We managed to get back to my friend Thom's house where I was living in Texas. As soon as we got there, we ran to Thom's spare room. She turned and pushed me onto the bed and gave me one of the single greatest blowjobs of my life.

The twist was that about 5 minutes into it she licked down the side of my cock to my balls then stuck her tongue in my ass. No warning what so ever, just BAM, instant contact with my naughty place that no one but a doctor is supposed to go. A few seconds after the fog cleared from what she had just done this wave of pleasure washed over me.

It was a struggle at first between the feeling of unnatural bliss and the shame that I was always taught to feel. Bliss won over by far trust me in this; do not listen to prudes or people who have never experienced something.

The only way to know if you like something or not is to try it, simple as that. I call it trisexual… I will try anything sexual once, twice if I like it. Just like when you were a kid with new food, sometimes you just have to just jump in and see, do not trust stereotypes or second hand knowledge when it comes to your body. No one knows you, your body, or what you will like the way you do.

Now as far as giving, it is hard to say which the best was, but I do know one that stood out. Yet another odd story, but my whole life is one odd story, so here goes; I was living with three gay men in a trailer in Texas and dating a young woman my age, I think we were 20 or 21 at the time. We were in the living room on the floor with a blanket under us and a blanket over us watching TV when like most times we laid together, things started to heat up quickly.

Our little hormones were raging since we first met and we frequently had sex 3-4 times a day every day. One of my roommates who we will call Bill was sitting in a chair across the room from the TV and about three feet from us. I started to play with her pussy while we were in a spooned position, which she always loved. She would start rubbing her ass back and forth and arch up and down to tease my cock. It always worked; I am a huge sucker for that one.

Without even taking her panties off, I just slid them to the side and she guided my cock into her. She was so wet and hot that all other thoughts of foreplay were gone. After only a couple minutes, she was squealing in ecstasy. The thought of Bill watching us, and the fact that I was hitting all the right spots turned her on. Out of nowhere, she stopped and pulled my cock out and aimed it up just a bit higher.

Without a moment's hesitation, she put my cock in her tight little asshole. With just a bit of hard breathing and muscle control on her part I was inside. Right here in front of my roommate I was deep in her ass. It felt so absolutely amazing. That was my first time having anal intercourse and I cannot describe another feeling quite like anal sex.

It only took a matter of minutes for me to cum, and it was all in her ass, she reached back and clawed my neck while reaching out to grab Bill's leg at the same time as she shuddered to orgasm. Bill could not believe how audacious we were being. Later on we all got a kick out of it, and told the story many times to our friends.

Finally, a tale that includes drugs, I know they are illegal and I am not telling you to go out and buy drugs or use them. However, there was a time when a woman at a party asked me to use a straw to blow cocaine into her asshole and I could not be rude and say no.

She quickly dropped her pants in the bathroom of a mutual friend's house, and handed me a straw already prepped with a good size bump of coke. Unceremoniously kicking away her black lace panties, she bent over and spread her ass cheeks apart, then began to finger her ass to open it up a bit for the straw.

I pressed the straw in and blew the coke up her asshole and she lit up like a Christmas tree. She squealed in delight or pain, maybe both I have no idea. Then she turned around and told me to take my cock out. She set a nice little line of coke across my cock and snorted it clean, then proceeded to blow me to get the residue. After a few minutes, she stopped, said thanks, and walked out pulling her pants back up.

Make sure you understand that even though this instance went well, just how badly this could have turned out. Without a doubt remember that people who use cocaine can have a heart attack or stroke, which can cause sudden death (DrugFacts: Cocaine, 2013). Cocaine-related deaths are often a result of the heart stopping known as cardiac arrest, after which the individual stops breathing (DrugFacts: Cocaine, 2013).

Other than the laws broken and moral compass failure there is one other thing to keep in mind during these situations. Your cock can go numb depending on how long the coke is wet and on the skin. Rather interesting experience for me but not one I would do again.

I am told that because the walls of the anus are much thinner the coke is absorbed almost instantly into the blood stream. That was definitely how it looked to me watching her. Cocaine hits the system extremely fast as it is, so anal usage isn't so much to get a faster responses but the sexual release with the bump of coke.

The degree of pain in anal sex is a mixed issue. In some relationships where bondage and discipline factors play a role, the pain your partner might experience in anal sex is part of the allure. For others, men and women often work carefully to decrease any pain, using lubricants and preparation, to increase comfort, and pleasure for both parties.

This takes patience and work, the special attention to ground work, serves as an intense form of foreplay, heightening excitement, extending the sexuality and sensuousness of the encounter, and, not incidentally, increasing the chances that the partner will have an orgasm, through the extended foreplay and stimulation.

Anal beads with multiple widths are a great way to build up momentum, as they start small and get progressively larger. Some individuals enjoy the sensation of the beads slowly stretching their anus, while others love the full feeling when all of the beads are inside them. Anal beads can be removed one by one or as one long strand of beads all at the same time during orgasm. Just be sure to add plenty of lube before inserting anal beads and wash them after each and every use (more on the care and maintenance of toys in chapter 8).

You have more than likely used a large portion of time learning about a female's orgasm places: How to find them, stimulate them, and how to turn a woman into a warm puddle of unintelligible pleasure with a G-spot orgasm. Men however, are generally less familiar with their own G-spot. Surprise fellas, some of you may be shocked to learn that the prostate is your equivalent of a woman's G-spot and yours is actually much easier to locate. I understand of course most men do not want to hear that; indeed the idea of exploring anal pleasure is supposed to be forbidden however, try maintaining an open mind and you can have an amazing orgasm.

Rules for men:

1. Never rush it, no matter if your partner is a brown eye champion or a first timer, never rush it.

2. Lube, Lube, Lube. I do not care what kind, or if its spit, or a generous amount of your partners own juices, but some type of lube!

3. Play with it first; give your partner some warm up, maybe a finger or two, maybe a toy. Bottom line know your partner well before attempting anal sex. I knew one woman who could fist her own ass. She loved it and somehow it was still tight around my cock (Don't judge just enjoy)

4. Slowly, gently ease the finger into the anus and wait for it to pucker over the finger before moving it in any further. When your finger is in to the first knuckle, make sure to check-in with your partner. How does this feel?

   Remind your partner to breathe slowly and deeply as this can affect the anal muscles. Tensing the anus and then letting go is a good way of learning to relax it.

5. Never ever go ass to pussy; it can cause infections that can not only be painful but cause permanent infertility. Clean it first or use a different condom than the one you used for vaginal sex. If you are with multiple partners or a new partner always, use condoms to protect you and your partner throughout the entire encounter.

   Rules for women:

1. If you want to control how slow or fast, easy or hard, deep or shallow, try being on top. That takes a lot of the anxiety out of what your partner might do or not do correctly

2. Breath, relax, talk your partner through it if it is not going right. It is your body, you will know better than they will.

3. If you want to do it to a man, add it into something, most do not like anal without it being introduced with a blowjob or some cock stroking. Hence the term "reach around"

4. Make sure your partner respects your limits and will not go deeper or faster than you are ready for. Go slow and make sure to 'call the shots' on the next level of penetration. The more you can trust your partner, the more relaxed you will be.

5. Never let your partner go ass to pussy, this can lead to infection. Make your partner wash off or use a condom.

6. The same rules apply as with the rules for men. If you are with multiple partners or a new partner, always use a condom and practice safe sex. This activity can easily cause Urinary Tract Infections, which cannot only be extremely painful but cause permanent damage to your reproductive health. Do not ever take a risk with your sexual health as it will lead to long term complications, that unlike with men can damage your ability to feel pleasure permanently.

Chapter 8: Toys

Toys can bring so much joy and fun into the bedroom (or wherever else you enjoy sex). Above all else, remember that they are not to replace, only enhance, or modify a sexual experience. Men who get penis envy over a toy are just sad little men with no self-confidence. Ironically, most of the partners who get jealous bought the damn thing in the first place!

I have a tote box full of toys to include several types of vibrators, ropes, cuffs, whips, and other assorted items to please my girlfriend. I have never become embarrassed because a girl had a toy, or asked for one. I am always on the lookout for something new to play with.

Toys allow so much diversity, like when I was away on business, Joan used to make me videos all the time with her favorite toy. I was never jealous and that thing got me off a hundred times watching her and her particular toys. She would change positions and scenarios, but the pleasure was always real.

When present with a partner toys can be part of every phase. Foreplay, during, solo work, group fun, anything really can be enhanced with toys. The sky is the limit so to speak. If sharing toys, please use protection. STD's are not above spreading through toys.

There are some made to pleasure both of you at once, like the ones you can find at novelty shops. My favorite of these is a cock ring with two different small vibrators on it, one above, and one below. The top one has little feelers on it so it tickles the woman's clitoris and the one below vibrates on a man's scrotum. This is just one example of the hundreds of types of toys out there. I will go briefly into different categories and some I personally recommend.

I have owned a plethora of toys in my life and I have never found a time where a woman did not mind them. Of course, I was careful about how much to show some of them because I knew they were not ready, but every woman I have known was at the very least open to the idea of toys.

I have built a couple of fuck machines for friends of mine in the past. I enjoy the process of construction, wiring, and programming of robotics or other machinery. Having the woman shop for a dildo or other attachment she wants on the fuck machine is fun.

I have never charged more than the cost of materials and generally get to watch women use the fuck machine the first time or two to make sure everything works well for them. I consider that a fair trade because everyone I see using one of my machines allows me to make better ones, or modify what they have to tailor more to their needs.

I love going to sex shops because I never feel uncomfortable, and the shady, sullen, creepy people just cannot believe how brazen I am in there. I grab toys, ask questions, debate with the employees on items but above all else, I have fun. Make sure you get what you really want, do not settle for less. This refers to toys as well as partners.

When shopping online, which can provide a wider variety of options, always be careful to read reviews and research all options. Never shop online unless you have researched not only the products but the company to ensure you are getting safe products. Nothing will ruin the fun more than using a product received online and you or your partner getting hurt in the process. Conversely, buying an item online and then having your credit information stolen through using a non-verified or secure website can take months to fix.

Dr. Ruth says, "Nothing will replace a relationship. Nothing will replace [when] you look at her with love and care, and that you really like being with her ... I don't want anybody to think that in order to have good sex and good sexual satisfaction, that they need any of this" (Dr. Westheimer, 2000).

Basic terms for sexual items include:

Strap on- a fake penis (dildo) attached to a harness that a female can "strap on" to penetrate another individual (Rader, 2009). This is the fake cock so that a partner can physically penetrate you or you penetrate them. There are many versions, some made for men as well as the standard ones for women. A good strap on will allow the wearer to be penetrated while wearing the device.

Dildos- a vaguely (or precisely) penis-shaped object used for sexual stimulation (Rader, 2009). These come in more sizes, shapes, and colors then anything I have ever seen at a store, it is the beanie babies for adults. The role it fills will determine a good amount of your choice. Also, be willing to branch out and experiment. You never know what might tickle your fancy so to speak.

I have collected several dildos, from small simple ones to specifically tailored 'G' spot vibrators. Even dildos that ended up being too big to be used I still kept anyways. Some people collect stamps, others baseball cards. I collect sex toys and instruments.

Whips- This covers everything from bull whips, riding crops, and cat-onine tails. Anything used to lash or gently tease the body with ends can fit into this group of fun accessories. I personally prefer cat-o-nine tails, the feeling of the lash across my back is fire, such pleasure with pain.

Clamps-There are dozens of different items both normal and specifically used for sex that can be found in stores or online. They offer a wide variety of pain levels, from barely notable to extreme. Even handy clothespins make for great clamps in a pinch (yet another bad pun).

Ropes- This is covered in depth in the bondage and advanced bondage chapters. I highly recommend hemp or nylon rope in 10, 15, 25 foot lengths with four, six, and 8-millimeter diameters. I have used dozens of other kinds of rope, in the end it is up to your personal preference.

Swings and saddles- If you have the room and an adventurous spirit these can add a completely new dynamic to any position and couple. A swing is a type of harness specifically designed with sexual intercourse in mind, where one partner is suspended, either above a bed or in a clear area, while the other has full access to their partner. All the same, there is a considerable variety; most common sex swings have a sling for the back, another for the butt and adjustable straps for each leg. Some versions are suspended from a bungee or spring to provide bounce.

Fuck machines- A device utilized to bring individual(s) to orgasm (Smith, 2008) such as machines designed to simulate sex or provide a platform to control larger dildos or other stimulating objects that require power or motion to function.

Rules for men:

1. Never get jealous of a toy, it is not your replacement. Check your ego at the door.

2. Have fun with it; add it into your arsenal. Make it a tool to aid you in your craft.

3. Toys are made for you as well as for her

4. Never mix partners with toys without using condoms or cleaning toys in-between. The health risk to yourself and your partners cannot be understated.

Rules for women:

1. Enjoy it, use it, and work it. Offer to let your partner watch and their eyes will light up.

2. You can use almost all toys on a man, especially the balls and or the taint (The piece of skin between the scrotum and anus which is sensitive)

3. Women who enjoy each other's company also have to be careful, your partner might not like what you do in the toy department, make sure to find something you can both enjoy, or have a few toys for each of you.

4. Clean and sterilize your toys between sessions and partners. Yes, you can give and receive STD's from other female partners.

Chapter 9: Toppings

This is for your kitchen borne additions to the bedroom (or whatever room you enjoy entertaining). Items found throughout include such wonderful flavors as whip cream, chocolate sauce, honey, ice cubes, and inanimate objects. I personally prefer honey to chocolate sauce because it is easier to clean. When honey gets wet, it dissolves, in my experience chocolate sauce is very messy. Messy can be fun but unless you want to stop and clean up the residue, it will get sticky and unattractive.

With this in mind, whip cream is a good steady staple of fun. Unless your partner is not dairy friendly then having whip cream around the house can never be a bad idea. There are lactose free brands of whip cream out there, if you do a bit of looking in case your partner is allergic.

Many people not just women enjoy a plethora of items that can be inserted or tactile items that can be found around the kitchen. Get creative and have fun, it is not just about the cucumber or warm apple pie. Get adventurous; you never know what item may become a knight in shining armor of passion.

When on the lookout for alternative sexual items, most can turn to the produce aisle for encouragement with many penis styled masturbation devices as close as the refrigerator, or fruit bowl (Fruit and Vegetable Vibrators, 2007). While the steadfast and loyal cucumber has always been there, there are always more options. These tips should help you get your daily servings of fruits and vegetables (Fruit and Vegetable Vibrators, 2007).

Some non-fruit favorites include Salami rolls, stirring utensils, bottles, and candles. Usually dull items with roughly round shapes to give the sense of penile penetration of some kind come in handy.

A Note on Safety:

Use common sense in any sexual activity. Before you play with produce, wash it thoroughly with warm water and antibacterial soap. If you are enjoying a harvest item vaginally, I strongly advise wrapping it in a condom to prevent damage to delicate areas of your body, and to help lessen the risk of anything getting "lost" inside you. I strongly recommended against anything pointy, like a carrot as this can cause damage to some very sensitive parts. Be very careful when inserting fruits or vegetables anally; they can become wedged in the rectum or lower bowel, requiring emergency medical attention and possible surgery to remove (Fruit and Vegetable Vibrators, 2007).

Be very careful if you are warming produce before use, a microwave should be used with extreme caution due to the interior of the item becoming hotter than the exterior, leading you to a false sense of temperature. Submerging the item in hot water is the preferred heating method. Ignoring these guiding principle can result in injury. The last thing you want is to go to the hospital with burns and having to explain it to a doctor.

Avoid shoving sugary foods anywhere. Do not use oil or oily foods, for that matter either, as they eat right through condoms, are great petri dishes for bacteria, and are total hangers on in your private parts, this includes unprotected bananas. Once you have finished a session with vegetables a shower is recommended to clean up any residue and avoid any health issues.

There are literally a dozen different fruits and vegetables that resemble a penis from which to choose. Finding the right one for you is as easy as shopping for dinner. Simply take a stroll down the fresh veggie section of your local grocer and find your next "meal."

A great example for men includes the slick flesh of papaya, combined with the smooth and slippery seeds creates a kind of sensation you cannot soon forget. Choosing a ripe papaya is tricky, you want it long enough to fit your penis but small enough to hold comfortably in one hand (Fruit and Vegetable Vibrators, 2007). Cut a hole in the round end of the papaya a little smaller than your penis, then do away with the majority of the pulp and loose seeds from within, leaving some along the sides to make ridge like contours (Fruit and Vegetable Vibrators, 2007). Enjoy your newfound homemade pocket pussy.

Vegetables can also be used to increase hormones. Asparagus is a good source of Vitamin E, making it a sexy little vegetable that increases your sexual hormones. The addition of a good supply of Vitamin A will help boost your sex drive to all new levels. All it needs is blanching in salted water for approximately three minutes and it is ready to go. To help keep it crispy and not soft and mushy dunk the asparagus in cold water right after. Asparagus goes well in different kinds of salads, risotto, soup, even casseroles.

Celery is another vegetable primarily for men; celery is reportedly ripe with two pheromones (androstenone and androstenol) which are emitted through an odorless secretion, alleged to be strongly attractive to women (Lizzy, 2008). When it comes to women, the same hormones can have encouraging effects on their energy and libido. For hundreds of years, raw celery root has been used as a medicinal treatment for impotence (Lizzy, 2008).

Nuts are high in the amino acid arginine, essential in the absorption of nitric oxide, a compound found in the body naturally, one of the many ingredients of the male erection. What's more, Lieberman states, "that nut oils are nowhere near as harmful as saturated fat or trans fats," (6 sex-boosting foods, 2014). Lieberman goes on to state that, "in fact, recent studies shows that nuts help reduce cholesterol," (6 sex-boosting foods, 2014).

"Plant foods are packed with nutrients and [are] low in fat," says Leslie Bonci, M.P.H., R.D., director of sports nutrition at the University of Pittsburgh Medical Center (6 sex-boosting foods, 2014). As a result, they help keep the arteries unclogged and help prevent both heart disease and erectile dysfunction (6 sex-boosting foods, 2014).

Tomatoes are a particularly powerful pick. "Studies show that the tomato component lycopene which is a member of the vitamin A family, helps maintain prostate health," says Shari Lieberman, Ph.D., a nutrition scientist and exercise physiologist (6 sex-boosting foods, 2014). Lycopene is best absorbed when tomatoes cooked in a little oil, as in a pasta sauce, so make some spaghetti and get "cooking" (6 sex-boosting foods, 2014).

Ginger gets some love for its ability to stimulate blood flow, which makes the erogenous zones much more sensitive. This also helps reduce a lack of rigidity in the penis for men, and the vulva for women.

Oysters are a shellfish that has a centuries-old reputation as a sexual potency food. Scientists laughed at this until it was revealed that oysters are also rich in zinc, which is necessary for men's reproductive and sex drive (6 sex boosting foods, 2014). Zinc is also an important balancing mineral for women.

Additionally, zinc has been linked to lessening the severity of colds and flu thus the proliferation of products like Cold-eez and Zicam. Nevertheless, eating them raw, you need to be careful, ensuring they are fresh and from clean water, or your evening of sexual entertainment might not be so entertaining.

Strawberries provide a superb amount of folic acid, which is a B vitamin that can prevent birth defects and, according to a University of California,
Berkley study, can result in a higher sperm count in men (7 foods for better sex, 2014). Strawberries are also full of desire boosting methylxanthines, chemicals that increase heart rate and blood flow and relaxing agents that help open blood vessels and loosen your muscles up.

Rules for men:

1. Keep it playful, have fun, do not take any of it too seriously.

2. Be careful and mindful of what you put where. The last thing you or your partner needs is to be the joke of the month at your local hospital.

3. Eat nutritious fresh or frozen fruits and vegetables to help maintain your physical and sexual health.

4. Make sure any insertable you use for yourself or your partner is clean. Do not jeopardize anyone's health in the pursuit of fun.

Rules for women:

1.   **Makes sure everything going in you is clean, there are a lot of pesticides and preservatives on fruits and vegetables that you do not need inside you.**

2.   **Always use condoms to ensure safety when possible; if you are allergic to something make sure that no compound or part of that goes near you or in you. Get an allergy test from your doctor if you are unsure.**
It is always better to be safe than sorry.

3.   **Your diet really can determine your sex life. Eat healthy and enjoy the benefits.**

Chapter 10: Simple Bondage

The key to healthy and successful BDSM play is communication, respect, trust, and safety. They are just like as in a healthy sex routine only compounded. In general, the results parallel, a deep association or link between you and your partner in both body and mind.

Dr. Freud was a pioneer among psychologists to address BDSM on a psychological level. Over a 20-year period, he explored the topic in many different ways. During this time his ideologies changed several times, nevertheless, he maintained one constant: BDSM was a pathological disorder (Freud, 1962).

Freud's idea was that people become masochistic was an outward expression of their desire to dominate others sexually (Freud, 1962). Freud goes on to say, "the desire to submit, on the other hand, arises from guilt feelings over the desire to dominate." Dr. Freud adamantly believed BDSM could present itself when an individual wants to take on the passive or submissive role, with the inherent acts within signifying their total submission to their partner (Freud, 1962).

In spite of the studies pointing towards BDSM not doing any real harm and not related to the pathology of a person, newer doctors of the field of psychoanalysis carry on the lingo using mental illness references when discussing BDSM. Sheldon Bach, Ph.D., clinical professor of psychology at New York University and supervising analyst at the New York Freudian Society, maintains that people are addicted to BDSM (Apostolides, 1999). "They feel compelled to be anally abused or crawl on their knees and lick a boot or a penis or who knows what else" says Dr. Bach (Apostolides, 1999).

"The problem," he continues, "is that they can't love" (Apostolides, 1999). "These individuals are looking for an emotional connection through BDSM. Deviant sexuality is the only way they can try to find love because they are locked into sadomasochistic interactions they had with a parent" (Apostolides, 1999).

In no way do I believe or feel as some of these comments you just read, it is merely a quote for educational purposes. I am trying to show all sides of the subject. Hopefully reading the varying opinions on this topic will help people understand the reasons this kind of stereotyping is outdated. You absolutely can feel love and emotional connections with partners, loved ones, and family if you practice an alternative sexual lifestyle.

Always keep in mind that the object of bondage is to confine or restrict without causing damage. A good bondage session can last hours and be a true delight for both the recipient and the host. It does not mean that it has to; I have been in sessions that were a mere fifteen or twenty minutes just because it was too intense of pleasure for my partner. To this day, I still think my favorite light bondage session has to be with a young spunky girl we will call Megan.

She and I used to have very vigorous sexual encounters together multiple times a day. We both enjoyed playing with others as well. She had short blonde hair, very perky 34C breasts, and a wonderful peach shaped ass. One such occasion was with a young Asian woman who Megan knew through her work. Megan and I agreed on all the terms such as I will discuss in the chapter: Threesomes and More.

I began the evening by cuffing Megan's hands behind her back while she was sitting doggy style. I used a leg spreader on her ankles so she would stay in that position with her legs a good thirty inches apart. Her young ass arched up in the air and the Asian woman we invited into the group used several toys on her while I alternated between some spanking and light clit play with a "rabbit." For anyone unsure of what a rabbit is, it's a small vibrator meant for outer play and some simple penetration (see the chapter on toys for a better description).

She came several times from the intense attention she was receiving and spent a good deal of time burying her head into the pillows. She thrashed around as much as she could and I had to put her upright a few times and hold her in place near the end.

This was a good session and afterwards the Asian girl felt comfortable enough and seeing the extreme pleasure Megan was getting from the attention, she wanted to try it. It is sometimes easier for a first timer to see it done on someone else first, both for the hesitation of doing it, and to see how it will work beforehand. I like to talk my partners through the experience when I tie them the first few times.

Understand the first time or two that you are bound; some people have a natural instinct of fight or flight. This is ancestral genetics telling you it is wrong to be bound in any form. That is part of the rush and enjoyment, the mind insists that it is wrong on a primal level, while the analytical side is lighting up with all the new sensations. Freely giving away control of your body can feel like free falling from a plane. There is no safety net once you let go, just a safe word (I do recommend safe words just in case).

I have witnessed someone go into a full-blown panic attack; on the other hand, I have seen a woman cream from multiple orgasms simply by applying restraints and a bit of rope. As in the case with this young Asian woman, this is why I enjoy this story above most others in the bondage category. Simply cuffing her and tying her legs with some satin handkerchiefs, I bought for such an occasion, that she came at least 3 times. There was so much cream and she was shaking so hard we had to stop there. Needless to say she was hooked and I got my nickname "knotty boy" after that.

If you are one of the people mentioned above, who have anxiety or panic attacks, I am not a doctor but I know a few tricks that can help (please see a licensed doctor if you have severe panic or anxiety attacks before attempting). Try just feeling the rope, laying it across your body; get comfortable with the way it feels on your skin. Slowly work your way into bindings. As soon as you start to feel an attack come on stop and breath until your comfortable again, then continue with the play.

You can perform bondage with a new partner or an old lover. If you are with a long-term lover or someone you truly feel an emotional connection with, spend the time after the bondage session has ended to complete the bondage experience. Do not let that exotic feeling end with the removal of the ropes. That time after is just like when you finished making love, the chemicals in the brain have changed but are still feel good reactions that can imprint your lover even deeper in your psyche. You can also ruin the encounter with insensitivity if you react as if the encounter did not mean as much to you as to the person being bound.

You can also practice with clothes on. To help both new practitioners of tying and the newly to be bound, this is always a good option. It helps build confidence in either partner. Trust is also easier to develop when you start slow like this. Sometimes with a new partner, you might want to play dressed first to see if they truly know what they are doing to ensure your safety.

Some great starter items for basic bondage include the following:

1. Cuffs- these come in several sizes and materials, I recommend starting with wrist and ankle cuffs. As far as material, the safer and less intense cuffs are made with leather but have fuzzy or padded materials on the skin side. This prevents rashes from skin irritation or chaffing. Handcuffs come in many varieties, from cheap knock offs to police handcuffs and some that work like shackles. It comes down to cost, design, and functionality.

2. Collars- same types of materials as your cuffs, also they can usually be found as part of a "kit", it is preferable if you can get all parts to a fun night to match. Collars are generally more for looks but can be used in conjunction with other bondage pieces. On the other hand, for the ones who enjoy being dominated this can be your "leash." You can tie into a collar when making different kinds of harnesses, or connect to a structure used for binding. I like to make the harness connection to the vagina when making a bikini line so that if you pull her head back it tightens on the vagina. This works two fold; one it causes mild choking for those that like it, two it teases the clit and vagina.

3. Blindfolds- very simple, you can use a shirt tie, rolled up towel, or just about any material handy. However, there are true blindfolds you can buy, like the ones worn on planes or sleep masks. The biggest complaint though is that most do

not stay in place, especially if you are going to be moving around. The best kind have an elastic band or chinstrap.

4. Rope- I strongly recommend hemp rope, solid braid nylon, or another soft material, they can get very pricey, but some starter ropes should not be a problem. Even though it seems like a lot, at least 100 ft. is my minimum. You will be amazed how fast you use up all your rope.

Rules for men:

1. Practice the knots before trying it on a person... do not be that idiot.

2. Make sure that your partner feels safe; you are much more likely to play again if you make them feel safe the first time.

3. Get either hemp rope or nylon-braided rope, which is easier on the skin, or some kind of restraints that will not damage the flesh. If you want to cause damage, go to the next chapter for advanced bondage.

4. See if you can do it mock, with clothes on if you're unsure the first few times, it should not be embarrassing to let her or him know you care enough to do it right.

Rules for women:

1. Mostly the same as men, if you are going to be doing the tying, do not think it is easy and the first time you will nail it right. Looking cute does not make up for bad knot work and pain or discomfort that can come with it.

2.   **If your interested hint at it to your partner, I have never met a man who was not at least intrigued by the idea of tying someone up.**

3.   **Become part of the experience if you are both out shopping, make sure it is your idea too, it will excite your partner to talk through what you want, and help steer the gear to your tastes. If you are going to be tied up, it might as well be by something you would want to be tied up with.**

Chapter 11: Advanced Bondage

This chapter is for the more experienced "knotty" people out there, or those interested in going further down the rabbits hole so to speak. In advanced bondage, there are more and less rules and restrictions. Advanced bondage is for those of you who have a natural pension for pain, or those looking for that next level. At no point am I saying that you have to have pain to be considered "advanced" merely that some truly enjoy the pain aspect.

This covers both the more aggressive style of S&M and bondage. They can be mutually exclusive or work together well; I will speak to both here. I have no quarrel what so ever for people that go to an extreme past my own personal experience, I am just speaking from mine. I looked for several years to find a partner that would make me have to say stop. I just never found one.

The first partner to bring me close to the edge was for her sake not for mine. She enjoyed fantasy rape, otherwise known as raptophilia or biastophilia (Association, 2013) to the point that I felt uncomfortable and finally had to stop seeing her. At first, it was fascinating and very exciting, but as time went on, I could not help but feel corrupted by it. I had to take a step back and evaluate myself mentally to see what was happening.

You see there are several forms of fantasy rape. With simply mild restraint and a little rough grabbing and removing just enough clothes for penetration on one end. Way at the other end is the kind that is literally controlled rape. She liked to be smacked around, forced onto a bed, usually on her stomach, and then held in place while her pants and panties were ripped or yanked down. She would try to fight back and yell no or beg me to stop, and when I stopped she would get mad and ask me why the hell did I stop.

From there, it was hard and rough penetration in her vagina and ass. She liked having her hair pulled and to be choked from behind very hard. The closer she came to passing out, the more she liked it. She was insatiable. This is why I am so in control during intercourse, to prevent a partner from going too far and harming themselves.

I have always understood the need for safe words and can usually tell when someone is being playful about stopping; however, I am also very sensitive to the psychological safety of my partners. She honestly sounded like she was being raped when we had sex. Every time was like this and I just could not want to rape someone. I was worried after a couple weeks like this that those acts might change my thinking and warp my sense of sexuality.

The sex was extremely exciting but dangerous, which of course was half the excitement. The violence and need to be brutalized was her way of playing out a series of traumatic events that occurred to her when she was young that she could now control. I just could not be that partner with her for an extended time because I was worried about enjoying it too much and loosing myself in that form of fantasy.

My next experience I would like to share was with a woman I never even had sexual intercourse with. It was a unique experience for sure. My friends and I were out doing a little club hopping in a college town one night. I came to meet a 20ish blonde-haired woman who was just cute as a button. We got talking and she had the same kind of attitude that I had, and in less than an hour, we were headed to her room. She hastily kicked out her roommate (She lived in a two roommate apartment on campus) and we got

hot and heavy quick. She confessed to enjoying pain and bloodletting.

This was a new experience for me so of course I was game right away. She climbed

on top of me wearing only a pair of panties and nothing else, while I had stripped my way

to just my cargo pants. She pulled out a razor blade from god knows where and proceeded

to ride back and forth, dry humping me while making tiny cuts on my chest until I was

bleeding small tear drops of blood.

She soaked her panties with cum while licking and then sucking the blood from the

cuts she had made. Eventually she was sated and offered to get me off in return. I thanked

her for the experience and called it a night, the rest of my evening I drove around town just

taking in what had happened and could not get her out of my mind. It was the strangest

sensations having someone drink my blood. The remaining nights we were there, I went

and saw her. She never wanted to have sex but simply to cut and drink my blood.

This is another instance where I need to stress caution. Sharing blood or drinking

blood from someone else is just as dangerous as unprotected sex. You can get a whole host

of sexually transmitted diseases without ever having sex with your partner.

This is one way to share yourself with your partner. Vampirism may be an erotic

experience for you or a partner. For some people, drinking the blood of your partner is an

experience to be shared. Regularly vampirism is seen as a deep bonding experience,

sharing the life force of you with your partner or your partner with you (Blood Letting and

Blood Drinking, 2009). It is often considered the ultimate way to share your life (or life force as some like to call it) symbolically with another. This consensual experience can be considered fantasy role-playing (Blood Letting and Blood Drinking, 2009).

Vampirism or the fantasy/curiosity associated therein has to do with the consumption of blood during an erotic exchange for sexual pleasure. At times, the partner's blood is extracted by controlled cutting, with teeth, or nails depending upon the level of intensity or role-play involved for those who are into more "rough" sex or a "primal" experience (Blood Letting and Blood Drinking, 2009).

A person bleeding oneself without ingesting blood is a type of auto vampirism known as auto-haemofetishism (Association, 2013). Cutters also fit into this category, the pain derived from the cutting releases endorphins, which can make a person feel high for a time. Some drug addicts resort to cutting in order to get that temporary high when other alternatives are unavailable.

The third experience I want to speak about is from a woman that let me practice my knots on her in the first place. Everything from simple braided knots to full on body harnesses and everything in between was open to her. She enjoyed being bound and helping me improve my craft. She was so much fun and helped me with fitting and tension.

She was a huge fan of how I wrapped her tits up; she had 42 DD that were the most perfect breasts I have ever seen on a woman. I just want to be clear on this, they were 42DD, and when she lay on her back, they did not fall to the side or sag anywhere. These were 100% real breasts and she was not a teenager. Her breasts were made for wrapping in rope, and they got the most delicious shade of red and purple. Her nipples would get all puffy from the squeezing process both from the ropes and from my hands.

Making a full body harness is time consuming and takes some practice to get the hang of. There are several pinch point areas to watch out for and always be cognizant of getting skin caught in the rope design. Leave a little slack around her vagina and thighs at first to tell if it is too tight or not, then simply adjust as needed to get the right amount of security you are looking for. It is the same for male partners except replacing the vagina with cock and balls.

Understand that even though breasts might turn red or purple there is almost no chance of actually cutting off the circulation, breasts are not a limb. There may be some discomfort at first but that passes quickly.

Make sure you know your partners general weight and size when using a swing or other form of support. Getting multiple sets if you are a host, a person with multiple partners, or just unsure who you are going to be sharing your playtime with is also recommended. It is very embarrassing to get a swing and cannot use it, or try to use it and the supports fail. Clean all equipment after each use. Proper care and storage will keep your toys lasting for a long time.

There is also an amazing series of internet videos at www.twistedmonk.com, they do a wonderful job to help people with the how and why of knot tying in bondage. They cover beginner to advanced knot tying systematically and the videos are very easy to follow while watching the demonstrations.

Spanking is a personal preference; everyone is different on how and where your partner would like to be spanked. For some, it is an event all in itself. To others it is a part of a greater sexual experience. You can use riding crops, paddles, and leather straps to spank as well as your open hand. There can be an increase in sexual gratification to the individual when you either allow them to see themselves being spanked or use blindfolds to take away their visual senses. Both techniques heighten the other senses often making the session that much more impactful.

I have always enjoyed getting my shoulders, back, and chest clawed. Some back whipping and biting certainly fall into my circle of desires as well, the sensation of pain and then the adrenaline rush following intensify the sexual encounter for me. Just like when I get a tattoo, immediately after all I want to do is have rough sex to burn off the hours of pain and adrenaline that comes with getting a tattoo done.

I personally love the cat-o-nine tails across my back. As hard as my partner can, either while I am bound standing or free but on my knees. Something about the subservient punishment plus the pain sends me to a whole other place. It actually clears my mind, like a kinky meditation.

Pinching and clamping can be as simple as clothes pins pinching the nipples or flesh around the breast, vagina, penis, scrotum, just about anywhere. There are several nipple clamps on the market that either support weight to pull on the nipples or vibrate them. Also, be mindful of the sensitivity of your partner, some like the pinch but need reduced pressure, others enjoy it as hard as possible. You can even get suction ones that swell the breasts and areolas.

There is a type of device that does the same thing for the vagina (commonly referred to as a vagina sucker). There is an outer cup shaped attachment intended to fit completely over the vaginal area. The suction forces the blood to the surface allowing the labia to swell, becoming engorged with blood and enhances sexual arousal. The more swollen the lips and clit become, the more sensitive they are.

Next, we will talk about swings and saddles. A good swing will require either a stand or mounting to a ceiling. If you have a place in mind and want to mount it, make sure to check for the location of your support beams. Not only are you supporting the weight of the swing but also the person who will be in it. This adds up quickly because you have to think about the force involved during your playtime.

A note on safety: make sure you check equipment before each use and be mindful during play. Eyebolts are the biggest issue I have ever heard of; they like to work loose or the support that the eyebolts are in break.

As far as saddles go, you can build a stand or just use it on the bed, floor, desk, anywhere you like. If there is a remote or plug in, then make sure a power outlet is nearby so that you aren't tripping over power cords or extension cables. You can also hide the cords under a small throw rug or carpet. Some saddles have attachments or accessories of their own. An example would be like a Symbian.

Masochists receive sexual gratification from a myriad variety of pain and or humiliating acts. Spanking, being whipped, made to perform humiliating acts, rude insults, blindfolded, disciplined, and restraints are all masochistic in nature (Rathus, Nevid, & Fichner-Rathus, 2004).

Sexual bondage is a part of bondage and discipline. Physically binding or restraining is most commonly called sexual bondage, where discipline refers to psychologically restraining your partner, such as through control, training, and nonphysical penalties such as with humiliation play (Ernulf & Innala, 1995).

I have spent a great deal of time studying rope bondage, tying partners of all different shapes and sizes. Even when teaching others how to safely perform artistic rope displays, I still learn something every time. Being open and communicating with others can be just as educational.

Rules for men:

1. Ensure that you keep a measure of restraint. No matter how it goes always work into bondage, don't start out at 100%

2. Swings and harnesses can be great, but make sure your partner fits and your support is able to handle the load plus action. The last thing you want is to embarrass or injure your partner while trying to have fun.

3. Never over due it, take breaks and drink water, don't shock them into never wanting to do it again.

4. If you are the one being tied up generally, you will be larger than your partner (not always), sometimes kneeling down, or lying down can help your partner(s) to tie you up.

5. Always agree beforehand how far this type of play will go. Do not under any circumstances deviate unless expressly asked for and agreed upon by your partner.

Rules for women:

1. Always ensure that trust is there, do not go into it half-assed or you will have a bad experience. If there is still trepidation then stick with bondage that is more basic or playing until you are comfortable.

2. If you are on the giving end make sure your partner is calm, excited, but calm.

3. There is usually a measure of control handed over or all control, take control, but do not abuse that control. Your partners trust can be a fragile thing.

4. Tying a man's genitals is just as tricky as wrapping a small-breasted woman, use smaller rope if possible, if not then start loose and tighten as you go.

5. If meeting a partner make sure you inform a good friend about where you are going and never engage in this type of play with a complete stranger especially in an unfamiliar place.

Chapter 12: Degradation and Humiliation

In this chapter, I will discuss some of the more extreme aspects of BDSM. Erotic humiliation is the consensual use of psychological humiliation for the erotic excitement or sexual arousal of the person being humiliated or the person doing the humiliating (Midori, 2005). This form of play can transpire in public or private venues.

Humiliation does not necessarily need to be sexual in nature, to receive the enjoyment just like several other sexual undertakings; these feelings received from the humiliation regardless of the actual nature of the activity are what the recipients seek. Generally, feelings of submission for the person being humiliated, and dominance, for the person doing the humiliation are the desired effects (Midori, 2005). These acts can be either verbal or physical in nature. Humiliation, unlike some sexual acts or desires, can be easily carried out over a long distance, especially over the internet (Midori, 2005). Humiliation is just one illustration of the environment possible in a Dominant submissive or master slave partnership.

Humiliation play can also be referred to as erotic embarrassment; this powerful aspect of BDSM play is often misunderstood. Despite misconceptions of average people, the submissive or recipient of the humiliation and or degradation has the power. The permission to be treated this way gives power to the submissive partner.

Generally, humiliation excites similar areas of the brain related with physical pain, in theory human brains evolved to remember rewards and punishments derived from social engagements as intensely as the reactions from physical reward or pain from outward stimulus (Midori, 2005). Just like any form of pain experimentation during sexual play, make sure both partners are consenting and responsible to ensure that the result is enjoyable, rather than someone becoming injured physically or emotionally. As an example, some partners may become sexually aroused or pleasured from the use of derogatory or insulting terms or phrases, on the other hand, certain terms can be truly offensive or destructive to the psyche of the individual receiving the humiliation (Midori, 2005).

From being walked like a dog on a leash in public, to stripped bare in a crowded bar and made to perform sexual acts for the pleasure of others, these are but two examples in a wide range of humiliation fetishes. For all of these acts both partners share in the humiliation play. They decide how far they will go, what can and cannot be said and done, even if it appears that only one of them is in charge.

Animal play, another form of humiliation is where the submissive is treated like a pet or dog play forcing the partner to eat and drink from dog bowls or something similar. Using terms such as words like slave, boy, girl, toy, and pet are considered verbal belittlement, follow along this same process. Adding insults and verbal degradation by calling the partner names such as tubby, ugly, stupid, or retarded. Derogatory names, such as tramp, bitch, whore, cunt, and twat. In addition, racial and ethnic slurs if that is what they prefer.

Negative comments of body parts and behaviors, such as demeaning comments of breasts, scars, ass, vagina, or cock continue the line of personal humiliation. Devaluing of such things as the way they walk, responsiveness, and personal hygiene. These are all examples of verbal humiliation.

Physical degradation includes but is not limited to; Ejaculating, spitting, and urinating on the submissive's body, especially the face including forced sexual acts such as; erotic massage, cunnilingus, analingus, and fellatio (Association, 2013). Erotic forniphillia is the objectification wherein one partner symbolically becomes human furniture, such as a footstool or bench (Association, 2013)(Turning a human being into a piece of furniture).

The psychology of humiliation play directly relates to sexual fetishism, given that normal seeming tasks may come to be sexualized by the association with arousal, these acts may be linked with exhibitionism in the sense of desiring strangers to witness or the sexual arousal due to individuals watching your sexual degradation (Association, 2013).

Undertakings like verbal abuse for some partners are a way of attaining the ego degradation or reducing sexual inhibitions. Such as homosexual couples using languages like faggot and dyke may be used. Still other humiliation role-play like infant play are shared with loyalty and care giving experience that these sexual fetishes can be seen as exercises in trust rather than just humiliation (Association, 2013).

Rules for men and women: (this list is gender neutral more than any other)

1. You must know your partners limits before hand. Do not ever take a new partner and just jump right into any kind of degradation.

2. Make a list and both parties need to agree, this is a form of contract that must be followed, any deviation must be initiated by the recipient.

3. The choice of public displays is a separate issue; just because you are willing to be degraded or humiliated in the comfort of your own home

does not automatically give your partner permission to do the same in a public setting. There are also public decency laws that come directly into play in any type of BDSM or Degradation play. Some towns have specific clubs for this; otherwise choose your public play very carefully. It could be a career ender.

4.   This play should never risk life, limb, or career for any sake.

Chapter 13: Building Your Own Play Room

This chapter more than any other, is wide open to debate and opinion. There is no right or wrong way to make a playroom. Every personality will create their own room their own way. Couples will make it functional and fashionable; each person will have special toys or pieces of equipment they prefer over all others.

Decorating a room just for sex can be a great bonding experience so to speak. In an ideal world, maintaining a room specifically for sex together is the goal. You do not really need a basement or a big storage room but it is nice to have enough space. However, you can always change things up in your bedroom if no other possibility is available. The goal is to make it deeply exclusive and personal to you and your partner.

When I first started exploring this type of lifestyle I had no idea how much really went into making a play room. I had seen other people's set ups, from simply having some toys under their bed or in the closet to a spare bedroom that the couple converted to a dungeon.

It was not until I began work on a playroom for my girlfriend and I that it really hit me. I was in for some serious work to make my fantasy a reality. Of course anything worth having is worth working for they say. Keep in mind your budget and time to work on the room. Do not get in over your head when you first start.

We have a full basement that is divided into three rooms; one is marked off for a bathroom, second is our full gym, and third was to be another spare bedroom but instead has become our playroom. This room is rather large and as I started shopping for items to fill it, I realized how daunting it would be. However, I have had so much fun I cannot stop getting more things. I was like a kid with a new room full of toys.

I set up suspension rigs attached to a metal support beam dissecting the center of the room, bought dark blue canvas to put on the far wall for camera backdrops, even furnished a nice simple bar stool in the middle of the room for certain scenes I wanted to play out. Of course, my girlfriend, bless her kinky little heart, immediately suggested we get a day bed and some other furniture to play on.

I bought a three-color laser projector, a strobe light (make sure your partner does not have issues with one, like having seizures), several black lights, and other assorted color bulbs for the room to set different moods. This affords us the opportunity to have many different kinds of sessions instead of just one or two variations on the same thing. My items might not be the same as what you like; I am just very visually stimulated and love technology, so that is fun to me.

Here is some advice on how to set up your playroom:

1.   Decide the feel and style you want the room to have. Romantic, erotic, or kinky no matter the taste, try to make the room feel like you do.

Choosing light or easy colors for romantic settings. Black, crimson, or purple for more erotic ambiance, these dark colors are good for your dark dungeon feel, the choices are endless. Never forget though, they are your choices, they should reflect upon you.

2.   You can have a comfortable bed, just try to avoid one too soft or does not squeak or make noises. The sound of a bed squeaking can be very distracting. You and your partner may prefer a more firm bed then you sleep in.

3.   Climate control is important; you do not want a room that is too cold. This will keep you from relaxing, and if you need to be under several layers of clothing or bedding, your options will be limited.

4.   If your going to have a sound system in the play room, then shop around and spend some money; a quality system will keep out unwanted noises out of the playroom, and gives you a more personal, private, fun environment (Sex Game: Decorating a Sex Room, 2008).

5.   Think about the light for the playroom. Most rooms in the world use normal, boring, functional light, instead of some romantic mood lighting in different colors (Sex Game: Decorating a Sex Room, 2008). I personally have two standing lamps with three sockets each and put different colored bulbs in each to help create different moods.

6.   Have some sort of storage for your toys, and other various sexual necessities. I prefer a shelf to lay out my toys so my partner can see what I have in store for her. Anticipation can be very exciting as well. You may want to have the option to lock the storage container when you are not using your toys. This prevents any embarrassment from accidental discovery.

7.   Last but not least, keep the room clean and remove anything that is not erotic, do not store junk or use it as a part time craft room (Sex Game: Decorating a

Sex Room, 2008). This room is for sexual games, adventures, and experimentation only if possible.

Just remember rooms are just like partners, each one will be different, make sure to experiment with a new room just as if you would a new partner. Take the time adjusting the light in your room until it is just right. Each room is going to be unique, so why do a half-assed job. The furniture that is in the room and how it is positioned will play a factor (Feng Shui). Be mindful of the height of the room if your going to set up a swing or suspension rig. There are very few "wrongs" in decorating; it is all up to what you are going for.

Be mindful of the sexual mood you are going for. Are you going for a feral night of abandon where damage to equipment or furniture is a potential risk? A more sensual encounter with some role-playing, props, and costumes? Perhaps a cozy lair with big fluffy pillows and bedding, comfortable enough to make anyone relax and feel safe, helping a partner let go of their inhibitions. Just remember, depending on the specific type of sexual feeling your going for will determine what type of lights you want to use (how to light a room for sex, 2006).

When doing the lighting for a room designed for sex, fluorescent lights are not the best choice. Most fluorescent lights are comprised of mercury; this toxin is unwanted especially in the playroom (how to light a room for sex, 2006). On top of these issues, fluorescent lighting is not the most stable light source and for some partners they might cause headaches and fatigue the eyes. In addition, fluorescent lighting does not spark sex appeal to a room in my opinion.

Lighting specific areas of the room will look more erotic then general lighting for the entire room. It is better to use many localized points of light. Get out a simple lamp, aim your desk light at the wall, try different things, and get imaginative with light up items you have around the house.

Use your lighting to flatter your body and the body of your partner. Perhaps try lighting from the side; it can really help highlighting the wonderful shape of your partners form.

Candles are great of course; they can help you set a romantic mood. I use the small floating lights in a little candleholder. I have colored ones that project an interesting flicker around the room; using paper shades is a great way to soften normal light bulbs to give a more seductive feel to your playroom. Use caution when using any type of open flame, and never leave open flames unattended.

You can create shadows on the walls with lampshades or cut out patterns on your lights to make beautiful sceneries. Using colored lights on a wall can create striking designs or place a light source so that you and your partners shadows are projected onto the walls around you, this "shadow play" can be intensely erotic (how to light a room for sex, 2006).

Make the room functional, able to be adapted to your needs. It does not have to be dark and brooding; your playroom is what you want it to be. Light stands with interchangeable bulbs and carabineers for your ropes. Making stands, crucifixes, and strap tables easy to assemble and disassemble can save space and give ideas for new ways to use them.

This room is absolutely yours to have fun in. Enjoy yourself and your partner. Be safe, confident, and sensual in all your sexual fantasies. As long as you follow your instincts and your heart, life will be good.

Chapter 14: Voyeurism and Exhibitionism

The objective of voyeurism is to witness unsuspecting individuals who are nude, in the course of undressing or engaging in sexual acts (Voyeurism, 2014). The individual who is being observed is often an unknown to the voyeur. The deed of observing or peering is undertaken with the desire of achieving sexual excitement, this voyeur most often is not attempting to have sexual contact or activity with the person under observation (Voyeurism, 2014).

Some voyeurs do not look for sexual release at all and if orgasm is sought, usually this is done through solo masturbation. The voyeur will either enjoy themselves during the voyeurism or after the session, depending on the memory of the sexual act or situation observed (Voyeurism, 2014).

This is the medical definition of voyeurism, however I use the term for people who enjoy watching others have sex or conduct sexual acts (with permission of course). We are not talking about illegal perverted sex offender stereotype but someone who gets consent from a partner or couple that enjoy being watched. This can also be known as scopophilia or scoptophilia.

Exhibitionism is a sexual desire defined by the urge to expose one's sexual organs to others, engage in sexual acts in front of others, particularly strangers. With consenting adults, it is perfectly legal and can bring a completely new level of excitement to the same sexual acts. This also includes autagonistophilia, which is the sexual gratification of being on stage or on camera.

There was a young woman in my life when I was just a teen that deserves a large portion of this chapter. Marci was the town sheriff's daughter and a real knockout of a redhead. She did farm work and loved horses, so of course she was naturally in great physical shape. This girl had an addiction to being almost caught. The closer we came to being busted doing something the more she loved it. Scared the hell out of me being a young teen screwing the sheriff's daughter, but add in that she loved to do it in public places or crazy crap in her parent's house and I was half-terrified most the time.

In public, our best moment was when we had sex on top of a moose… Let me clarify, it was an 8' plastic mascot in front of an ice cream store. Late fall temperatures in the north are not very conducive to the lack of clothing in which she preferred. It all began with the conversation of strange places to screw (one of her favorite past times). These conversations always ended badly (or great depending on your perspective) and she would get very worked up quickly.

After the ice cream shop closed and all the customers had moved on, she broke her plan to me. Apprehension played across my face for just an instance and then a huge stupid smile. Marci began taking off her clothes as she walked over to the mascot. Without another thought, I followed, doing the same as quickly as I could.

She laid back on the mascot and precariously I got up on the rump of this plastic sex base. We fucked for about 10 minutes until someone pulled into the parking lot. We ran off laughing uncontrollably with whatever clothes we could find. A car horn honking and someone yelling at us about being "damn kids" and threats of police being called was all that followed us.

She also enjoyed having me over at night while her parents were home, watching a movie or T.V. She would say she needed something from the kitchen, and drag me off into the other room. Then with me facing the back of her parents head from the kitchen, she would try to blow me, flash her tits, or stroke me. I do not know how we never were caught, and her dad did not kill me.

That relationship was short lived because she was always looking for the next high and the next thing. I just was not enough for her, she wanted more and more risky distractions, and I knew where it would end. I do know at some point she was finally caught and her father all but locked her up in jail.

Another instance was during a plane ride I took from Boston, MA to Portland, ME. The flight was a red eye in the middle of the night on a tiny 16 row puddle jumper. Being one of only four people on the plane that were not crew, it was sure to be a dull and quite flight. Boy was I in for a surprise. Once the plane broke through the clouds, the only flight attendant on board buckled into her seat in the back of the plane and went to sleep.

A few seats in front of me was a grey haired older woman who was fast asleep. The second other passenger on board was to the right and front of the grey haired woman and he seemed asleep as well. The third passenger however was wide awake and the center of this story. She was a good-looking, short, blonde-haired woman who could have passed for a cheerleader.

I was looking out the window on my side at the moon; it was huge and very bright. The young woman was across from me on the other side of the plane trying to see the moon as well. I asked her if she would like to sit in the seat beside me so she could see better. She smiled and popped up out of her seat and climbed over my legs to sit down near the window.

We commented on the view briefly and the emptiness of the plane. A wicked smile came across my face and I asked her if she had ever fooled around on a plane. She grinned back and shook her head no. Quietly and carefully, she slid down the sweat pants and panties she was wearing and I pulled out my cock from my pants while grabbing my emergency wallet condom.

Looking around to make sure everyone was still sleeping she climbed onto me reverse cowgirl style. Slowly and with as little movements as possible, we got it on right there in row 15 seat C of that little plane. The thrill that at any moment someone could wake up and see us, or hear her moans and know what we were doing excited us both.

We finished up just before the ding sounds and lights came on signifying we were about to land. She hopped off me and buckled in the seat when the flight attendant came by to let us know to prepare for landing.

After the plane landed and we got off, we made our way to the luggage carousel where my girlfriend and her boyfriend were waiting to welcome us home. As each of us hugged our significant other a quick wave and wink was all we would ever share again between us.

While this was a fun event for a young man, know that it could have had consequences even though we practiced safe sex. Sex in public places is something to be given careful consideration especially when you could wind up in jail because of it. With current air travel restrictions, I would not recommend this type of activity.

As for watching others have sex, I have had the pleasure of wonderful friends that shared a passion for parties and swinging. In the past I have planned a good number of swinger parties and group parties between friends. On some occasions, I was allowed to be there solo strictly to help new couples and keep the night moving along for less experienced couples that wanted to be good hosts. I have also watched women together simply to study lesbian acts.

I had a roommate once who allowed me to watch her encounters and photograph her. We worked at a local bar together where she was a bartender and I was a bar back. We never did anything together but had a lot of fun collecting memories.

It all started with her wanting to take some pictures for her boyfriend. I had a couple different cameras at that time and more than enough willingness to accommodate her. The boyfriend really loved the pictures and understood how close she and I were. My roommate and I were both open in our life style choices so everything played out well.

Also, remember voyeurism can include simply having a mirror in the room, such as on the ceiling, or even a full-length mirror. Watching yourself, or seeing a different view of the same act can be a huge turn on for both of you.

This brings me to the last part of this chapter. With technology has come a completely new way to enjoy voyeurism and exhibitionism. The webcam, what a fascinating tool for sex this device can be. When used legally, responsibly, consensually, and safely it can be a wonderful addition to an existing relationship and another way to maintain a safe yet gratifying relationship with a partner.

Just make sure you know with whom you are chatting. There is nothing worse than having a skumbag on the other side of the conversation trying to exploit you. Thousands of sleazy people out there want nothing more than to get you naked and then show everyone else with him that you do not know about. Make sure you are comfortable with being put out there before you go through with nudity across the internet.

This is another moment where trust is everything. In this new technological age, more and more people are getting reckless with sending photos and videos across the internet or cell phones. Be careful please, once something is out there it cannot be taken back. Keep that in mind or end up like all the exploited "stars" out there.

Rules for men:

1. Do not ever let someone watch without your partners consent. This is much more an issue with men than women; it's not cool and illegal in most states.

2. Each time you watch or are watched make sure to get permission, just because you were given approval once does not mean it is ok every time.

3. Anything put in any format online is out there forever. If you do not want your boss, friends, or mom to see it; then do not click the upload button period.

Rules for women:

1. I make it very clear for men, but women need to be just as aware that letting someone watch requires your partners consent as well.

2. Remember that there are boundaries for everything. Watching and being watched, in person or across the internet, rules need to be established for each instance separately.

3. The same that applies for men; anything put in any format online is out there forever. If you do not want your boss, friends, or mom to see it; then do not click the upload button period. I can not stress this enough.

Chapter 15: Threesomes and More

In this chapter, I will be speaking to group sex with or without your primary partner. For most cases, this is meeting up with a pair of people from the opposite sex, or a group of people that you happen to end up in just the right circumstances. Sometimes it is a once in a lifetime experience that you never thought possible and for others it is the development of situations.

It can be a matter of all the planets aligning or the moon being at just the right point. Any number of reasons that people can come up with to explain how it was possible. In reality there can be no reason or all the reasons, you can make it happen, or let it happen. Hustler and Penthouse do not own the monopoly on great sex stories. You can make your own.

What I mean by this is how many times in your life have you had "what if" moments? Where the desire was there, everything feels right and then you or the person you were talking to has to leave, or you simply walk away. When you feel that moment take a chance, the worst thing that can happen is they say no. Pull the trigger figuratively, "he who hesitates, masturbates."

I have had more than a few partners that enjoyed having sex with multiple individuals. It can be a world of fun as long as it is known as that. I cannot stress enough at this time about safe sex. The more partners you have, the greater the risk of sexually transmitted diseases. Be responsible to yourself and your partners. One mistake can have devastating consequences for any of your future partners without you ever showing any symptoms at all. Do not risk it, always practice safe sex period.

I have a story that needs to be told that shows the danger of not doing it right, or for the wrong intentions. This experience changed my life forever; my ex-fiancé left me, and cost me a great friend all at the same time.

I was engaged to a woman many years ago and living with my friend Mike. We went out one night to the city fair with the intent of getting Mike laid. Allow me to elaborate on this; Mike was a great person but very shy and at 22 had never been with a woman in his life. I took it as my personal mission to fix that.

Half way through the evening, we were in line to get on a carnival ride that my fiancée was afraid to ride. When Mike and I got on the ride called the Zipper, we sat down beside a young blonde-haired woman wearing only a white wife beater, trashy jeans, and she had bruises on her arms and back.

As we were buckled into our seats, I looked over at the girl, introduced myself, and then made sure to introduce Mike. Mike waived at her and mumbled as usual. I did everything I could to make Mike the center of attention to no avail.

After a few minutes of Mike not trying, I took over and began laying out the groundwork for what I thought for years afterwards was going to be an epic night. After the ride ended, we went to a pool hall and began drinking and flirting exceptionally. I was honestly trying to get this girl interested in Mike but to no avail, he just seemed to have no alpha male in him at all.

After a very short couple of games at the pool hall, we went back to my place and really got the night into action. A bottle of Jack Daniels and a piss poor game of strip poker later (which no one was trying to win) and we were naked in the bedroom. Now mind you I was young and not making a lot of money at the time so the bedroom consisted

of a box spring/mattress on the floor and a nightstand with a lava lamp.

I was going down on my fiancé when the blonde-haired woman said how she wished

she were getting something like that. I looked over at Mike from between my fiancés thighs

and he was just sitting in the corner, naked, drinking from the bottle of Jack. I told him to

come and get her and he just mumbled something about drinking.

My fiancé looked up at me and told me to go for it, so naturally I did what any good

host should do and began playing with the blonde-haired woman as well as my fiancé. We

swapped around a bit and I ended up fucking the blondehaired woman. Meanwhile my

fiancé grabbed Mike, laid him on the bed, and all but raped him. Several hours later, I had

gone between both girls several times and Mike was passed out. A week later Mike left, he

and I never talked again, he moved across the country and I had no idea why until very

recently when Alicia finally explained it to me.

For years I had thought I did a great deed for Mike by getting him laid and making

his first experience a foursome no less! I did not get how bad it could have affected him,

and that most people are not like me. I feel bad now and hope someday he knows how

sorry I am for that. I lost a good friend for a single night of carnal pleasure.

So please make sure all parties are interested before going down that path. It might

seem like a great idea now, and stuff that penthouse and hustler write about, just think for

five seconds, and make sure no one will get hurt in the process.

My original introduction to the woman known as Megan in my book is another

cautionary tale that needs to be told. It began with her dating a female friend of mine whom I used to do engineering projects with. She was brilliant and a lot of fun just to hang out with. She was gay and was dating Megan however did not do much physically with her.

One day we were at Megan's apartment and the two of them were tickling each other on the couch when suddenly Megan jumped on my lap throwing her arms around my neck. She giggled pleading with me to save her from her girlfriend. Her girlfriend lunged at us and the tickling became petting, which became fondling, until things got very serious.

I assisted her girlfriend with moving Megan to the bedroom and then quickly took her pants and panties off. I was not allowed to remove my clothes out of respect for Megan's girlfriend. She did not like the look of a cock and had no interest in seeing one. I instead assisted her in teasing, toying, and eating out Megan. We made her orgasm so hard she fell off the bed and crawled into the closet to hug her stuffed animal and shiver in the fetal position.

When Megan had finally recovered, we spent the remainder of the day driving her wild repeatedly. We tied her up, used various objects on her, and generally had our way with her.

After that day, it became almost a daily event with the three of us together until one day something changed. I did not see the signs at all or I would have stopped, but at some point, Megan fell for me and ended up leaving her girlfriend to be with me more permanently. As much as my friend told me it was fine and that she was happy, I knew it hurt her.

My friendship was never the same after that, we grew apart and hung out less and less over the months. I have let my libido destroy so many good friendships and relationships for that matter. No matter how glamorous and exciting some of my stories seem, I know I left a trail of hurt feelings and lost loves along the way. Now that I am older, I really do see the consequences of my actions as a youth. Just be careful and mindful of what you are getting for what you are giving up to get it.

Rules for Men:

1. Do not ignore one partner over another. Make sure all partners feel important.

2. Talk beforehand about what is and not off limits.

3. Jealousy is not an option during these sessions, the second that feeling creeps in step away, breath, and talk to your partner before something happens.

4. If you are the one stepping into a couple that has been together, make sure that there is equal attention and that you let the couple enjoy themselves with you.

5. Consent from all parties is essential.

Rules for women:

1. Reinforce with your lover how they are still your primary, how they were better than the one you brought to "play" with. Keep egos fed.

2. Enjoy yourself, do not be a pawn, be a queen in your experiences.

3. It doesn't matter the make up of the group, all women, two women and a man, or you with two other men, keep to your rules and what makes it fun for you.

4. **Safety is extremely critical. I cannot stress enough how much damage can be caused by not practicing safe, sane, and consensual sexual acts.**

Chapter 16: Swinging

This can make or break a relationship depending on the reason for the "swing." It can be a number of reasons from simple boredom in the bedroom to the excitement of doing something "naughty." No matter the reason, there are certain guidelines to help make your experience a successful and pleasant adventure. Important things to remember for both partners; if you come as a couple then leave as a couple, do not make a solo play, which is not swinging.

Remember that these kinds of parties are not degenerates with disgusting whorehouses; courtesy and good behavior gets you invited back, or makes your party the one to attend. Civility is still important, even to swingers. These parties share all of the same themes as a regular party; bring a host gift, RSVP invitations whether you are going to attend or not (it keeps you on the list if you answer them), you always have the right to say no, always. Do not be afraid to use a friendly smile and say "no thanks" or if you are the one being told no, have the respect and courtesy to understand and walk away.

Swingers interviewed all say their intimacy is more intense during sex because they encourage their partner's sexual fantasies. Both partners are so confident and open in the relationship that distrust is not an issue. Swingers swear that cheating is not an issue because the relationship is already in an open state, having sex with another individual as long as their partner's consent. However, this is an act that must be agreed upon because some couples that get into this type of lifestyle self-destruct.

Swinging is often defined as the covenant between husband and wife to have sexual intercourse with other partners, in a setting where they both engage in sexual behavior usually at the same time and place (Fang, 1976). What is emphasized in almost all swinging is the mutual consent between the couple, knowledge of the arrangement, and approval of the new partner or partners (Fang, 1976). Co-marital sex, group sex, partner exchange, and keying are common terms. Mate, spouse, and wife swapping are some of the other terms known to describe this type of arrangement.

Some couples in open marriages fancy different types of sexual relationships. Marriages that prefer extracurricular activities emphasizing love and emotional involvement have a "polyamorous" type of open marriage (Fang, 1976). On the other hand, couples who prefer agreed upon extramarital relationships with more need of sexual gratification and recreational sexual partners have a swinging type of marriage. If you go out and cheat on your partner you are not a swinger and there are other issues that need to be worked out.

These differences may be influenced by psychological factors like sociosexuality and can add to the creation of polyamory and Swinging communities (Fang, 1976). Despite these differences, all open marriages share common difficulties: the lack of social acceptance in their family or community. The most critical keys to maintaining the relationship as a couple in my opinion is the need to manage jealous rivalry.

I was good friends with a husband and wife while living in Texas who wanted to become swinger hosts but had no idea how to go about it. They were still fairy new to swinging and had only been to one other party. They both agreed they would feel safer and more comfortable if they hosted parties versus going to unfamiliar places and being out of their element.

We immediately went down the list of simple things needed to make a good swinger party.

1. A large enough space to comfortably accommodate the number of couples expected.

2. Multiple areas advantageous to sexual position and privacy if desired.

3. Possible themes and games to help entertain and make it a fun atmosphere.

4. House rules of what they were willing to do or have done at their party. These rules are then sent out to guests via email before the day of the event.

Their home was more than large enough for the party. They had a den with a large sectional and a pair of love seats plus two spare bedrooms with beds so the sexual places were nicely covered. Of course, strip poker and Hawaiian shirt night played well for their first event. This opened up good foods and music to entertain early in the evening (most swinger parties do not start with you walking in the door and people having sex everywhere).

Before they ever held a party though they asked me to join them in a threesome to help calm their nerves and to make me feel like part of their group. I think it was more getting over nerves for both of them because this was all still very new to their marriage. We kept it very light and playful and I guided them through some fun events that they were unaware of.

When the time finally came for their party, everything was a huge success. We pit roasted a small pig and did some chicken on the grill, four couples joined them for the evening and no one left unfulfilled. The mark of a great party is the responses the following day; they received raving reviews from all the couples.

My friend's parties became a monthly event that no one wanted to miss.

After their second party, they felt much more at ease and began going to social events held by other couples. The development of confidence in their relationship and the acceptance into the community of swingers grew together and made their relationship even stronger.

Rules for men:

1. Enjoy your experience and if your spouse wants to hear about it then tell her, if not keep your mouth shut and respect her decision. Some women find it exciting; some want you to have a good time but do not want the details.

2. Use protection when not with your partner; do not bring home more then you left it with.

3. If you are a host, make sure everyone else is happy and taken care of before you should think about your own needs. Check in with your guests from time to time.

Rules for women:

1. Make sure it is what you want too; if this is just for your partner then it is going to end badly. Maybe not the first or second time, but it will end.

2. This is your time to set ground rules, all the power is on you when it comes to swinging. Your partner is likely to agree to just about anything.

3. If you are the hostess, greet at the door, take coats, make introductions, show people around, and after everyone is comfortable and things are going well, then and only then should you proceed to find fun for yourself.

4. Women in this type of lifestyle are at very high risk for HPV, which can lead to cervical cancer and Urinary Tract Infections. Protect yourself and ensure you and your partner both understand the health risks involved.

Chapter 17: An Act too Far

"La mort d'amour," the French phrase for "love unto death," that dying during sex is the ultimate expression of love. Sometimes, even with the best intentioned and precautious partners, bad things can happen. Now if you add in the potential risk of a random partner being mentally damaged or unstable and you have real risks. This chapter will cover things that can go wrong, what you can do to help minimize those risks, and be aware of the possible outcomes.

The first and one of the scariest I can think of out there from my perspective is 'bug chasing' and 'pozzing'. These two slang terms have to do with the practice of individuals participating in unprotected sex with partners who are known to be HIV-positive with the intent to contract the HIV virus themselves (hence the name 'pozzing' deriving from the word positive) (Mark Griffiths BSc, 2013). The participants of this deviant practice are known as "gift givers", infected persons that knowingly have unprotected sex to transmit the HIV virus. Despite how hard it is to believe the practice could possibly be true, scholarly research confirms the existence of this sexual practice (Mark Griffiths BSc, 2013).

Continued research suggests a multitude of reasons for why people would attempt to intentionally contract the HIV virus. In a 2004 paper in the British Journal of Social Psychology, Dr. Michele Crossley reported some people point toward the practice as extremely exciting due to such a high-risk behavior (Mark Griffiths BSc, 2013). However, most of the reasons involved with these cases suggest the partners do not actually want to contract the HIV virus; they enjoy the fear and excitement of the chance to become infected. This same article also pointed towards some bug chasers appearing to simply being lonely, desperate individuals who are trying to get themselves infected so that they will be given the attention, nurturing, and support they feel they deserve or owed somehow. Similarly, some of these individuals see the contracting of HIV as a way to become a member of a community that prompts public sympathy and caretaking (Mark Griffiths BSc, 2013).

Safe and consensual sex, which I preach about often throughout this book, should be screaming at you after reading the last report. Please use protection, and if you are not, then get tested and have your partner or partners get tested regularly. If you both choose not to, that is your choice, but if your partner simply makes excuses about not using protection or claims allergies, there are forms of protection that are made specifically for allergy sufferers. If they say the sex is not as good or does not feel the same, then ask if they would rather not be having any at all. Take that moment to do the right thing, all it takes is one time to change your life forever.

Next I will discuss erotic asphyxiation otherwise known as breathe control play. This is the intentional reduction of oxygen to the brain for sexual pleasure. Psychologists have also described the sexual practice as asphyxiophilia, autoerotic asphyxia, and hypoxyphilia. A gasper is the common term for an individual who participates in these acts. The erotic interest in asphyxiation is known as a paraphilia in the Diagnostic and Statistical Manual (Association, 2013).

Death usually results from loss of consciousness produced by partial asphyxia leading to loss of control over the means of strangulation. Even though asphyxiophilia is usually combined into sex with a partner, some enjoy this behavior alone, called autoerotic asphyxia, this can be dangerous as it becomes harder to get free from accidents. Victims of these terrible accidents are usually rigged to some sort of "safety release mechanism" that did not work like expected as the individual lost consciousness.

Peter Anthony Motteux was an English author, playwright, translator, publisher, and editor of The Gentleman's Journal. Mr. Motteux died from apparent autoerotic asphyxiation in 1718 (Peter Anthony Motteux, 2004), which is the earliest reported case that I was able to find.

With a good partner, there should always be safe nonverbal ways to let them know to stop, or they should have the sense to stop before it becomes harmful. Asphyxia play can be great fun, I personally love being mildly choked and have had a dozen partners who enjoyed being choked at varying degrees. Control is the important factor. One of you needs to be mindful of what you are doing to keep you both safe.

The next subject to discuss is sexual cannibalism; this is considered a psychosexual disorder. This involves an individual sexualizing eating the flesh of another person. Sexual cannibalism is thought to be a form of sexual sadism and is linked with the act of necrophilia (Association, 2013). People who are sexually excited by the idea of being eaten, eating another person, or observing this process for sexual gratification are known as vorarephilia, (Paraphilias , 2014).

I think it should be very clear why this particular game might not be so fun to play, but for anyone not sure, biting, licking, and sucking is fine. However, having chunks of flesh removed or organs cut out of you is detrimental to your health. Unless dating

Hannibal Lector or Jeffrey Dahmer is your thing, then I strongly advise staying away from these chat rooms and personalities.

Conclusion

In conclusion, I hope you can take something from this book and apply it to your own sexual experiences. If even one aspect of your life is improved because of this book then I have done everything I had hoped to accomplish. All I have ever wanted is to take away some of the horrific encounters people come talk to me about.

Safe, consensual, fun sexual experiences are the goal. Take care of yourself and your partners. Do not bring bad experiences into the play, and never ever start a session in the wrong frame of mind.

I get so upset when individuals come to me and tell me about all the lame, sorry excused, and pathetic sexual experiences they have had because all there partner did was pump for 2 minutes, cum, then go to sleep or leave.

That cannot be man's sexual legacy; you need to take pride in what you do for your partner. You should see that look in your partner's eyes that screams "holy shit, what the hell was that?" Regret should not be the first feeling your partner has after you finish.

It is not just men however; women do not get off that easy (no pun intended on that one). Laying there unmoving like a warm pastry is not the extent of your involvement during intercourse. If that has been your sex life, then do something about it. If your partner has not given more, or wanted more, it is your obligation to make a change.

Instead of complaining to your friends or co-workers, do something about it. If your partner is unreceptive to your needs and desires maybe it is time to find a new way to communicate your desires. Sometimes being blunt is the only way, just being mindful of how you speak as not to hurt your partner's feelings.

Keep that smile because you know something most average people do not. Each experience is your dirty little secret, but a good dirty little secret. Something that no one can take away from you and that gives you power over your life. Even when out of control, you are in control.

Stagnant and stale sexual experiences make you stagnant and stale. Have you ever known a person who had amazing sex all weekend then came to work Monday not glowing and appearing giddy? There is a reason for that...

I have learned a great deal in my life from these experiences, some good some bad. The lessons I have learned make me a more compassionate and caring lover today. It is not all about me; it is ultimately about the experiences I share with someone I care about very deeply. That is my greatest hope of what this book can do for you. Everyone deserves a better sexual experience.

Glossary

Polyamorous relationship- To be polyamorous means to have open sexual or romantic relationships with more than one person at a time. People who are polyamorous can be heterosexual, lesbian, gay, or bisexual, and relationships between polyamorous people can include combinations of people of different sexual orientations. People in polyamorous relationships may or may not be married, although people who identify as polyamorous tend to be rejecting of the restrictions of the social convention of marriage, and particularly, the limitation to one partner.

Paraphilia- A paraphilia is a condition in which a person's sexual arousal and gratification depend on fantasizing about and engaging in sexual behavior that is atypical and extreme (Paraphilias , 2014). A paraphilia can revolve around a particular object such as children, animals, underwear or around a particular act like inflicting pain or exposing oneself. Paraphilia is far more common in men than in women. The focus of a paraphilia is usually very specific and unchanging. A paraphilia is distinguished by a preoccupation with the object or behavior to the point of being dependent on that object or behavior for sexual gratification (Paraphilias , 2014).

Salirophilia- A sexual arousal gained from in some way dirtying or messing up a partner. The partner is usually attractive and the sexual gratification arises from actions such as covering them in filth, messing their hair, or tearing their clothing even though generally, no violence is involved (Salirophilia, 2014).

Mysophilia- A pathological interest in dirt and filth, sometimes with sexual manifestations or a paraphilic sexual arousal that hinges on dirt or being covered in filth (Paraphilias , 2014).

Bibliography

50+:Live Better, Longer Can Good Sex Keep You Young? (2014). Retrieved from WebMD: http://www.webmd.com/healthy-aging/features/sex-keep-young?page=2

6 sex-boosting foods . (2014). Retrieved August 10, 2014, from MSM Healthy Living: http://healthyliving.msn.com/health-wellness/men/sex/6-sex-boosting-foods#2

7 foods for better sex. (2014). Retrieved July 29, 2014, from Health: http://www.health.com/health/gallery/0,,20307213_3,00.html

Apostolides, m. (1999, September 01). *The Pleasure of Pain.* Retrieved from Psychology Today: http://www.psychologytoday.com/articles/199909/the-pleasure-pain

Association, A. P. (2013). *Diagnostic Statistical Manual of Mental Disorders* (5th ed.). Arlington, VA: American Psychiatric Publishing.

Blood Letting and Blood Drinking. (2009, Mar 12). Retrieved Jul 18, 2014, from Gothic subculture: http://www.gothicsubculture.com/blood-drink.php

Dr. Westheimer, R. K. (2000). *Encyclopedia of Sex (second edition).* Continuum Intl Pub Group.

DrugFacts: Cocaine. (2013, April). Retrieved from National Institute on Drug Abuse: http://www.drugabuse.gov/publications/drugfacts/cocaine

Ernulf, K. P., & Innala, S. P. (1995). Sexual bondage: A review and unobtrusive investigation. *Archives of Sexual Behavior Volume 24, issue 6,* 637.

Fang, B. (1976). Swinging: In retrospect. *The Journal of Sex Research,* 220-237.

Freud, S. (1962). *Three essays on the theory of sexuality.* Avon: Harper colophon books.

Fruit and Vegatable Vibrators. (2007). Retrieved August 03, 2014, from Homemade Sex Toys: http://www.homemade-sex-toys.com/vibrator/)

how to light a room for sex. (2006, June 10). Retrieved July 15, 2014, from About.Com Sexuality: http://sexuality.about.com/od/tipstechniques/ht/sexlighting.htm

Ley, D. j. (2011, February 06). *Back Door Psychology.* Retrieved from Psychology Today: http://www.psychologytoday.com/blog/women-who-stray/201102/back-door-psychology

Lizzy, L. M. (2008, December 28). *Women, Sex and Vegetables.* Retrieved from SOCYBERTY: http://socyberty.com/sexuality/women-sex-and-vegetables/

Mark Griffiths BSc, P. C. (2013, March 14). *Contractual arrangements: A brief look at 'bug chasing'.*

Retrieved August 24, 2014, from DRMARKGRIFFITHS:
http://drmarkgriffiths.wordpress.com/2013/03/14/contractual-arrangements-a-brief-look-atbug-chasing/

Merriam-Webster's Dictionary and Thesaurus. (2014). Merriam-Webster, Inc.

Michael J. Formica, M. M. (2009, January 8). *Gender Differences, Sexuality and Emotional Infidelity.* Retrieved July 29, 2014, from Psychology Today: http://www.psychologytoday.com/blog/enlightened-living/200901/gender-differencessexuality-and-emotional-infidelity

Midori. (2005). *Wild Side Sex: The Book of Kink Educational, Sensual, And Entertaining Essays.* Daedalus Pub Co .

Paraphilias . (2014). Retrieved July 27, 2014, from Psychology Today: http://www.psychologytoday.com/conditions/paraphilias

Peter Anthony Motteux. (2004). Retrieved from Spiritus Temporis: http://www.spiritustemporis.com/peter-anthony-motteux/life.html

Rader, W. (2009, August 31). *Definition of.* Retrieved from The Online Slang Dictionary: http://onlineslangdictionary.com/meaning-definition-of/strap-on

Raine, A. (2013). The Anatomy of Violence. New York, NY: Pantheon Books.

Rathus, S., Nevid, J., & Fichner-Rathus, L. (2004). *Human Sexuality in a World of Diversity (6th Edition).* Allyn & Bacon.

Roy, S. (2008, September 08). *The Psychology of Desire.* Retrieved August 03, 2014, from EzineArticles: Article Source: http://EzineArticles.com/1764341

Salirophilia. (2014, June 17). Retrieved July 27, 2014, from Right Diagnosis: http://www.rightdiagnosis.com/s/salirophilia/intro.htm

Sex and Aging. (2014). Retrieved July 29, 2014, from WEBMD: http://www.webmd.com/healthyaging/guide/sex-aging

Sex Drive: How Do Men and Women Compare? (2014). Retrieved July 29, 2014, from WEBMD: http://www.webmd.com/sex/features/sex-drive-how-do-men-women-compare

Sex Game: Decorating a Sex Room. (2008, Aug 08). Retrieved Jul 18, 2014, from Articles Factory: http://www.articlesfactory.com/articles/sexuality/sex-game-decorating-a-sex-room.html

Smith, B. G. (2008). *The Oxford Encyclopedia of Women in World History, volume Kaffka.* Oxford University Press.

Voyeurism. (2014). Retrieved July 27, 2014, from Encyclopedia of Mental Disorders: http://www.minddisorders.com/Py-Z/Voyeurism.html

WEBMD. (2014). Retrieved july 09, 2014, from 10 Surprising Health Benefits of Sex: http://www.webmd.com/sex-relationships/guide/sex-and-health

www.ingramcontent.com/pod-product-compliance
Lightning Source LLC
LaVergne TN
LVHW061330060426
835513LV00015B/1342